Relational Psychophysics in Humans and Animals

Relational Psychophysics in Humans and Animals offers a comprehensive overview of the often fragmented field of psychophysics. It introduces key concepts in psychophysics and clearly summarizes and illustrates the central issues through telling examples. It combines empirical research and theoretical approaches from general psychophysics, animal psychophysics and developmental psychophysics to create a systematic comparison of these three key areas. Throughout, Viktor Sarris makes a strong case for more comparative psychophysical research across different species and across different stages of development. He presents original research and examines frame-of-reference models, behavioural psychophysics, developmental psychophysics, perceptual-cognitive psychophysics and evolutionary perspectives, to create an integrated framework for the direction of new research. The book will be an invaluable aid for researchers in the fields of perception and psychophysics.

Viktor Sarris is Professor of Psychology at J.W. Goethe University, Frankfurt.

Relational Psychophysics
in Humans and Animals

A comparative-developmental approach

Viktor Sarris

Psychology Press
Taylor & Francis Group
HOVE AND NEW YORK

First published 2006 by Psychology Press,
27 Church Road, Hove, East Sussex, BN3 2FA

Simultaneously published in the USA and Canada
by Psychology Press
270 Madison Avenue, New York NY 10016

*Psychology Press is an imprint of the Taylor & Francis Group, an
informa business*

© 2006 Psychology Press.

Typeset in Times by RefineCatch Ltd, Bungay, Suffolk
Printed and bound in Great Britain by TJ International

British Library Cataloguing in Publication Data
A catalogue record for this book is available from the British Library

Library of Congress Cataloging in Publication Data
Sarris, Viktor.
    Relational psychophysics in humans and animals: a comparative–
developmental approach / Viktor Sarris.—1st ed.
        p.   cm.
Includes bibliographical references and index.
ISBN 1–84169–569–6 (hardcover)
1. Psychophysics.   2. Psychology, Comparative.   I. Title.
    BS237.S33 2006
    105.19'.8—dc22   2006

ISBN 10: 1–84169–569–6 (hbk)

ISBN 13: 978–1–84169–569–6 (hbk)

For Anja, Irma, Roswitha and Sonja.
More than ever.

Contents

Figures

Tables

Preface

In this book an integrated overview on research in *relational* psychophysics in humans and animals is presented – from a comparative-developmental point of view. Although rich in theoretical conceptions and suggestions as well as in experimental findings over many years, the present field of research is still lacking in coherence. Therefore, the author's task here has been to integrate the largely separated theoretical notions and respective experimental facts coming mainly from human adult psychophysics, but partly also from developmental psychophysics with either human infants or animals. Indeed, I consider it as both urgent and timely to provide a more integrated treatment of perceptual-cognitive approaches in psychophysics, to compare the more promising human and animal work with one another – largely from a biopsychological perspective – and to point to needed psychophysical research projects, also from an evolutionary point of view.

The author has been involved in issues of comparative-developmental *"context"* (frame-of-reference) work for more than three decades. However, mainly during the last ten years I have developed a growing interest in a multiple-stage theory of perceptual-cognitive processing going along with the establishment of psychophysical behaviour, both in humans and animals. More recently, within several symposia – at the *International Society for Psychophysics Meetings* held in Strasbourg/France (2000), Leipzig/Germany (2001), Larnaka/Cyprus (2003) and Coimbra/Portugal (2004) – the ideas and findings of this research have been discussed more fully. The Introduction provides an outline of this monograph.

Acknowledgements

Both in my research and in writing this book the inspiring exchanges with many colleagues and friends, including the late Professor Mario Bunge (Philosophy, Montreal) during his visits to my laboratory in Frankfurt, have been very fruitful. I have also benefited from several earlier exchanges with Norman H. Anderson (Psychology, San Diego), Morton E. Bitterman (Comparative Psychology, Honolulu), Sheila Chase (Comparative Psychophysics, New York), Hans-Georg Geissler (Psychology, Leipzig), Robert

A.M. Gregson (Psychology, Armidale/Australia), Eric G. Heinemann (Comparative Psychophysics, New York), Gert Haubensak (Psychology, Giessen), Friedhart Klix (Psychology, Berlin), Allen Parducci (Psychology, Los Angeles), Irvin Rock (Psychology, Berkeley/California), David R. Thomas (Psychology, Boulder/Colorado), and Friedrich Wilkening (Psychology, Zürich). Furthermore, I acknowledge the gracious support by the Deutsche Forschungsgemeinschaft, Bonn-Bad Godesberg, for several extended research grants (1968–1989).

Special thanks are due to various colleagues and friends who – more recently – discussed with me ongoing controversial issues of comparative psychophysics and thus helped to improve my thinking on several issues in this book, namely: Bill Angermeier (Furnish-Lettermullen, Ireland), Stuart Anstis (San Diego), Jürgen Bredenkamp (Bonn), Nicola Bruno (Triest), Walter E. Ehrenstein (Dortmund), Petra Hauf (München and Frankfurt/M.), Michael Kubovy (Charlottesville, Virginia), Kaoru Noguchi (Tokyo), Tadasu Oyama (Tokyo), Giulia Parovel (Padova, Italy), Michele Sinico (Bologna, Italy), Lothar Spillmann (Freiburg/Brsg., Germany), Lawrence M. Ward (Vancouver), and Eugene R. Wist (Düsseldorf). Fortunately, Stuart Anstis is co-authoring Appendix 3 of this book ("An Engine Model of Relational Psychophysics"). Various colleagues have read the book chapters and checked its quality, namely Walter Ehrenstein (chapters 1, 2, and 5), Gert Haubensak (chapter 5), and Petra Hauf (chapter 4), and two unknown reviewers. Regina Kressley-Mba and Lawrence M. Ward read all chapters twice and improved the last version of the whole book. I am extremely grateful for all this valuable support. However, it goes without saying that the remaining errors or shortcomings of this monograph are mine.

Over many years my research in animal and human psychophysics was made possible through the reliable cooperation of my junior colleagues and technical assistants; they all helped the work go rather smoothly, day by day. Gertrud Carabalí did most of the secretarial work and Siegbert Reiß, together with Jeanne Schnehage-Poci, helped to finish many of the PC Microsoft scripts and figure graphs. Thank you so much.

Finally, I am indebted to my friendly animal playmates, namely the Greek cat Matta, the German cocker spaniel Trixi, and the baby chick Gogo for having shown me that it is worth studying their lawful perceptual behaviour and minds, including their amazing memory capacity as well as their other remarkable psychophysical skills ("awakening cognition").

Viktor Sarris
Frankfurt
November 2005

Introduction

Purpose and scope of this book

Central to the concern of modern psychophysics is the notion of perceptual-judgemental relativity, contrary to the mainstream and more traditional approach of sensory psychophysics during the nineteenth and twentieth centuries. Take for example the loudness of familiar sounds varying in intensity, say from the absolute threshold of hearing to the painful noise of a jet plane take-off. Although the variable acoustic events are consciously experienced as "absolute" they are in fact "relative" to their immediately given contextual background, at least partly. In general, humans and other animals do not directly identify single stimuli but compare each stimulus event in relation to other stimuli, all of which involve both simultaneous and successive (sequential) comparison processes beyond simple sensory event recording. Psychophysical judgement is, therefore, a complex task, which is nowadays better understood through the combined use of different but interrelated perceptual-cognitive paradigms.

In this book the basic concepts of a *frame-of-reference* (*FR*) psychophysics are illuminated, together with a quantitative model of *transposition*. Thereby, the relevance of a behavioural psychophysics approach with human and animal subjects is exemplified, in light of systematic comparative experimentation. Tentatively the evolutionary impacts of this interdisciplinary approach are also shown. The association of major areas of investigation, which are typically unrelated to each other (research myopia) – especially those of comparative psychophysics, relational learning and memory, as well as developmental perception – will be demonstrated.

The following topics and questions of a *relational* psychophysics are treated in the current text:

- *Relational perception and epistemology* (chapter 1). Some basic philosophical implications of human and animal perception and cognition are outlined, with special emphasis on the relational basis of perception and psychophysics. Question: Are there viable bridges between traditional gestalt-oriented approaches and modern perceptual-cognitive psychophysics?
- *Frame-of-reference models in psychophysics* (chapter 2). Three major

frame-of-reference (FR) models, including those with different assumptions and research strategies, are described and evaluated, namely the adaptation-level model, the range-frequency model, and the similarity-classification approach. Question: What are the advantages and disadvantages of these concepts and other kinds of current research in perception and psychophysics?

- *Behavioural psychophysics: Contrasting ideas and findings* (chapter 3). By means of a general model the fundamentals of behavioural psychophysics and transposition are outlined, thus offering the experimental rationale of comparative perception and psychophysics. Some major findings of the author's and his junior colleagues' investigations are presented in light of other research results. Question: What general conclusions can be drawn from the present human and animal research in relational psychophysics?

- *Developmental psychophysics* (chapter 4). The former comparative ideas and findings are extended to some basic age-related work in human and animal psychophysics. The author's and his students' more recent research results obtained with humans and young birds are described and evaluated. Question: To what extent may these comparative developmental findings enrich ongoing and future work in relational psychophysics?

- *New perspectives on relational psychophysics* (chapter 5). This chapter provides a more theory-oriented treatment of relational psychophysics. In particular, a multiple-stage idea concerning the different processes involved is outlined, including the notion of perceptual-cognitive psychophysics – also in respect to cognitive neuroscience. Question: How should present-day and future research go beyond the piecemeal orientation of the earlier approaches in psychophysics?

- *General discussion and conclusions* (chapter 6). In the concluding chapter on relational psychophysics an attempt is made to relate the respective research approaches to the principles of "perceptual constancy" and "perceptual memory". Here it will be demonstrated that future experimentation should be guided by an interdisciplinary account, thus trying to overcome the arbitrariness of past fragmentary research agendas. Question: What lines of future work should be followed, and will a biopsychological and neural-network approach in psychophysics support the respective demands?

The three appendices at the end of this monograph contain the crucial methodology of past and future research of this kind of comparative psychophysics; namely, the description of the major apparatus used in animal research (*Appendix 1*), the presentation of some mathematics of transposition and psychophysics (*Appendix 2*), and the illustration of the so-called *engine model* of the bird's relational psychophysics (*Appendix 3*).

A useful introductory book for teaching students about psychophysical research methods and theory may be consulted in order to appreciate the virtues and benefits of the present text (e.g., Gescheider, 1985; Bruce, Green, & Georgeson, 1996). Some of the major lines of thinking here are at least partly related to the following reference works:

Bremner, J.G. & Fogel, A. (Eds.). (2001). *Blackwell handbook of infant development*. Oxford: Blackwell.
Chalupa, L.M. & Werner, J.S. (Eds.). (2004). *The visual neurosciences* (2 Vols.). Cambridge, MA: MIT Press.
Kaernbach, C., Schröger, H.E. & Müller, H.H. (Eds.). (2004). *Psychophysics beyond sensation: Laws and invariants of human cognition*. Mahwah, NJ: Lawrence Erlbaum Associates, Inc.
Nadel, L. (Ed.). (2003). *Encyclopedia of cognitive science* (4 Vols.). New York: Nature.

Kaernbach et al. (2004) presents a series of theoretical and experimental studies that expand the general principles and laws well beyond the classical domain of sensation. This work also contains an updated overview chapter on various frame-of-reference models in psychophysics (Sarris 2004; see here chapter 2).

An important collective (multiple-author) source for the bird's visual cognition is provided as follows: Cook, R.G. (Ed.). (2001). *Avian visual cognition*. Retrieved January 2004 from http://www.pigeon.psy.tufts.edu/avc/toc.htm

Thus, the comparative analysis of the relational psychophysics of "transposition" behaviour is of central concern. Whereas chapters 2, 3 and 4 emphasize the empirical basis, the remaining chapters 5 and 6 contain the more theoretical perspectives of this book.

1   Relational perception and epistemology

> As a matter of philosophical principle, mathematical argument can never tell us, by itself, what the status of nature is. The state of nature can only be discovered from empirical observation.
>
> (Laming, 1997, p. 10)

Introduction

In this chapter on the epistemology of perception and relational psychophysics some basic philosophical questions in the domain of both human and animal perception and cognition are dealt with, namely:

- epistemological implications of perception and cognition
- relational perception and cognitive psychophysics
- the evolutionary perspective on comparative perception.

Modern accounts of the history of psychophysics are provided elsewhere (e.g., Murray, 1993; Murray & Bandomir, 2001; see also Algom, 1992, 2003; Boring, 1942; Link, 2003; Sarris, 2001a, 2004; Sommerfeld, Kompass, & Lachmann, 2001).

Epistemological implications of perception and cognition

The concept of relativity, or relativism, refers to the epistemological principle that all physical and phenomenal events have meaning only with respect to some global or systemic properties that are emergent relative to their components that the latter lack (see Bunge & Ardila, 1987, Figures 5.1, 5.4, 5.5; pp. 90, 101–103). It is important to keep the epistemological, physical and phenomenological "relativity" meanings as fundamentally different from each other.

For example, in his posthumous book *The World of Parmenides* (1998), the philosopher Karl R. Popper (1902–1994) emphasized the point that already in ancient Greece some of the pre-Socratic thinkers made the fundamental distinction between philosophical and psychological *relativism*, like Xenophanes of Colophon (about 570–480 BC) in Asia Minor (see also Gold, 2003; Levine, 2003; Nagel, 1995; Norris, 1997; Putnam, 1988). This basic distinction is important in the sense that *psychological relativism* refers to the organism's behavioural and mental activity of all kinds, whereas *philosophical relativity* – doctrine of relativity – denotes a sceptical theory of epistemological inquiry (e.g., knowledge of what things really are is impossible because of the human mind's basic subjectivity).

Clearly the present monograph deals with psychological and not philosophical relativity and concentrates on a particular type of relativity, namely on perceptual-cognitive relativity.

In the context of social psychophysics it is tempting to assume that ethical relativity in everyday life might be based on perceptual-cognitive relativity. Note, however, that ethical relativity is another world from biophysics or biopsychology. It refers rather to philosophy or metaphysics or religion (Allen Parducci, personal communication, August 2005; see Mussweiler, 2003; Parducci, 1995; see also Rorty, 1991). Interesting as this speculative conjecture is, not only for psychology, it is beyond the scope of this book.

Phenomenology as a guide to behavioural and brain research

Phenomenology is a term related to the scientific study of immediate experience ("appearance") as the basis of perceptual psychology. Its focus here is on subjective events as one experiences them. However, there is no attempt made to disregard or deny the physical and chemical reality of objective events, but the basic issue for a phenomenological approach is to avoid the exclusive focus upon the objective, i.e., non-subjective reality (see the illustrations provided by Figures 1.1 and 1.2).

The importance of phenomenology for perceptual research, emphasized by gestalt psychology, has hardly seen more creative proponents than Max Wertheimer (1880–1943) and Gaetano Kanizsa (1913–1993). Through careful observation and artful variation of visual phenomena, Wertheimer and Kanizsa – together with their colleagues and students – revealed the puzzling and intriguing richness of perceptual appearance. Indeed, phenomena are immediate (*direct*) and undeniable facts of experience and hence a prime source of scientific investigation. Their systematic observations and descriptions are fundamental in the light of the respective state of knowledge about sensory and brain functions as well as of the physical properties of the stimulus relationships (e.g., Ehrenstein, Spillmann, & Sarris, 2003).

Phenomenal description, however, is just the starting point of modern perceptual research and far from being self-sufficient (Figure 1.1). Besides the "phenomenological mind" there are nowadays also the neurobiological and computational approaches (Kubovy, 2003; see also Cruz, 2003; Spillmann & Ehrenstein, 2004). Closely related to this fundamental issue is the concept of "gestalt" as an emergent property (e.g., Bunge & Ardila, 1987; Kubovy &

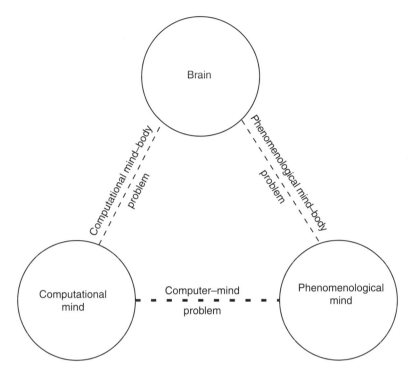

Figure 1.1 Three epistemological gaps: phenomenological, brain-based, and computational issues in comparative perception and psychophysics. The diagram
illustrates the three main theoretical facets of cognitive sciences today and
their debated linkages, i.e., comparative neurobiological science ("brain"),
cognitive psychology ("phenomenological mind"), and computer science
("computational mind"). The explanatory gaps between these three
approaches are indicated by the broken lines (see especially the "computer–
mind problem": in bold dots). Sceptics claim that the explanatory gaps are
unbridgeable (adapted from Kubovy, 2003).

Gepshtein, 2003). In comparing human and animal perception with each
other, one has to rely on the systematic study of behavioural observations.
Such research, which must be guided by sound phenomenology, illustrates
one of the explanatory gaps (Figure 1.1; see also Nagel, 1974, 1995, 1997).
Combining phenomenal approaches with neurophysiology must not be
confused with neurophysiological reductionism.

After all, phenomena in their quality are independent of the knowledge
of the brain processes underlying them (admittedly, the broken lines in
Figure 1.1 illustrate the fundamental *explanatory gaps*). In other words,
percepts do not become deprived of anything if they are "consulted" by
neurobiological experts in order to understand the functional processes that
subserve them. Epistemologically, phenomena per se can rather serve to

broaden and deepen the understanding of brain functions since they may give us the primary clues of why things "look" as they do (e.g., Mausfeld, 2002; see also Koch, 2004; Kubovy & Gepshtein, 2003).

The argument here is in favour of a wider scope of phenomenology, traditionally resident in philosophy and psychology, to enrich the perspectives of a modern *gestalt psychophysics* as tightly linked to behavioural and brain research. In fact, there is nowadays an increasing dialogue between the neurophysiological and psychophysical approaches so that with David Hubel, the renowned neurobiologist, one may hold that "gradually we are coming to understand each other's language and are mastering each other's techniques. The field has become immeasurably richer" (Hubel, 1995; quoted after Ehrenstein et al., 2003, p. 452).

Relational perception and cognitive psychophysics

As implied by the introductory statement, the term "relational" (from the Latin *relatio*) refers to the notion that the physical and biological stimuli and events never exist and function in isolation, but always interact profoundly. This epistemological postulate is highly significant in principle, and it is of particular relevance also to psychology, starting with the (sub-)fields of perception and psychophysics.

Gestalt psychology and the stimulus-ratio concept

Both historically and systematically the relational approach in perception and psychophysics has been promoted mostly by gestalt psychology (Ash, 1995; Murray, 1995; Sarris, 1995, 2004, 2006; see also Spillmann & Ehrenstein, 2004). Its basic idea is illustrated by a host of well-known qualitative and quantitative examples (see Kanisza's now classical demonstration in Figure 1.2). Note that current comparative research findings suggest that Kanizsa's well-known subjective contour perception holds alike for human infants and adults as well as for monkeys, cats, and even baby chicks (see Lea, Slater, & Ryan, 1996; Regolin & Vallortigara, 1995, 2003; Slater, 1998, 2001; von der Heydt, Zhou, & Friedman, 2000; von der Heydt, Friedman, & Zhou 2003).

As a matter of fact, comparative studies on gestalt perception in, say, the mouse and the young chick illustrate that Kanizsa and his students (Kanizsa, Renzi, Conti, Compostella, & Guerani, 1993; Regolin & Vallortigara, 2003) have rightly pointed to the general holistic (relational) character of perceptual-cognitive behaviour, in line with the findings of the classical phenomenological research in humans (see also Goldstone, 2003; Kellman, 2003; Pomerantz, Portillo, Jewell, & Agrawal 2003; Watt & Phillips, 2005). For example, Lucia Regolin and her co-workers, Padua (Italy), demonstrated amodal "completion" and "occlusion" effects in the young chick; namely, baby chicks reared with a partly occluded triangle preferred a complete triangle rather than a

Figure 1.2 Subjective contours: two examples of the so-called Kanizsa patterns (illusional triangles). After fixating the two drawings for a few moments one "sees" a white phantom triangle, its basis is either at the bottom (*left*) or on top (*right*). Note that the subjective contours are perceptually real although physically absent (see Figure 1.1).

fragmented one during the test phase (Regolin & Vallortigara, 1995, 2003; see also Ushitani, Fujita, & Yamanaka, 2001).

The ratio principle

A fundamental case of the relational approach in perception and modern psychophysics is provided by the quantitative ratio principle (for a selective overview see Sarris, 2001a, 2004, 2006). For instance, a given response is said to be relational in correspondence to the respective stimulus ratio used in perception (e.g., see *Wallach's ratio rule* in lightness perception as supported also in the study by Chien, Palmer, & Teller, 2003 with human infants). According to Hans Wallach, a former student of Wolfgang Köhler (1887–1967) and Max Wertheimer during the 1920s and 1930s in Germany, the general assumption for lightness constancy states that the perception of surface lightness is based on the weighted ratio between the focus light ("figure") on the surface and the light that is reflected from its immediate surroundings ("background"; see Cataliotti & Gilchrist, 1995; Gilchrist, 1990, 1994; Gilchrist & Bonato, 1995; Rock, 1977, 1990, 1996; Sarris, 2001b, 2004, 2006; see also Actis-Grosso & Vezziani, 2003; Epstein, 1977; Gogel, 1972, 1977, 1998). Another classic example for the ratio principle, as a fundamental perceptual phenomenon of relational learning, is the *transposition* effect (Figure 1.3; see also below, the *evolutionary* perspective on comparative perception). The full theoretical impact of transposition is described in chapter 3.

Ratio rule, similarity and belongingness

Whereas the ratio rule in sensation and perception constitutes an important principle of comparative psychology, it is not meant here to be exclusive: namely

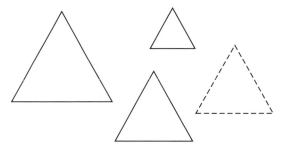

Figure 1.3 Transposition figure: size or contour (dotted vs. straight line) does not change the perceived shape of the "triangle" (*left*). Note that the transposition phenomenon is based on the physical and subjective similarity of the target triangle (e.g., dotted lines) and its smaller (or larger) variants. (Adapted from Rock, 1996.)

perceptual-cognitive judgements are assumed to be based on both relational and "absolute" factors of *similarity* and *belongingness* (Epstein, 1977; Gogel, 1977; Rock, 1977; see also Hahn, 2003; Kellman, 2003; for more on this issue see chapter 4). The following two examples should illustrate – *pars pro toto* – some further issues as to the present state of the art in perception and psychophysics (Ehrenstein et al., 2003).

Signal propagation from the edge – filling-in

Computer simulations using different spatial filters demonstrate that much of the stimulus information in a visual percept is contained in the contour of a figure. We not only see stick figures, but we also have access to uniform brightness, colour and texture that fill the enclosed surface area. How is this surface information represented in the visual cortex? Recent research corroborates the following idea (see DeWeerd & Pessoa, 2003). Unless the contrast of a stimulus is above threshold (absolute or differential), gestalt factors cannot act on it: i.e., in order for perceptual principles to become effective, there must be something to work on (the figure will not emerge on a background when its contrast is too low, e.g., subliminal). Therefore, the first requirement for seeing is a supra-threshold contrast of the stimulus (see also Hamburger, Prior, Sarris, & Spillmann, 2005; Parovel & Vezziani, 2002; Pessoa, Thompson, & Noe, 1998; Spillmann & De Weerd, 2003).

Geometric-optical illusions

Figure 1.4 illustrates some well-known geometric-optical illusional figures. In the author's research group, three different types of geometric-optical distortions were investigated: (a) the distance or gap illusions, known as the Delboeuf illusion; (b) size or extent distortions, known as the Baldwin illusion; (c) the Ebbinghaus-Titchener illusion, which belongs to the "mixed"

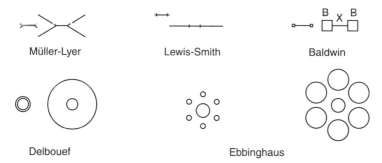

Figure 1.4 Some well-known geometric-optical illusional figures (here called more precisely optico-geometric distortions, OGD configurations). On top are the classical "contour" patterns (Müller-Lyer, Lewis-Smith, Baldwin figures); at the bottom, left, is a "gap" pattern (Delboeuf; at the right is a mixed-type figure, i.e., Ebbinghaus-Titchener). (Adapted from Sarris, 1986.)

type of *optical-geometric distortions* (*OGD*; see Ehrenstein et al., 2003; Gregory, 2003; Sarris, 1986). Both the distance (*D*) and the surrounding context-size (*B*) may be systematically varied together with the focus stimulus (*X*) to be judged. This is schematically illustrated here in Figure 1.5 for variable contour size *B* and distance *D*. The experimental data have supported these predicted nonmonotonic trends of the illusion (see also Ehrenstein, Hamada, & Paramei, 2004; Hamada, Ehrenstein, & Paramei, 2003). In passing, it should be added that the similarity principle has been demonstrated to be important also in other optico-geometric illusion work (for more, see chapter 2; see also Coren & Enns, 1993; Coren & Miller, 1974).

Remarks

The two above-mentioned examples illustrate the empirical basis of the potential linkages between visual experiences, comparative behaviour, and arguably (e.g., Ehrenstein et al., 2003, 2004) brain activity. The examples can be extended further to include such prevailing gestalt factors as *proximity* and *similarity* (see Medin, Goldstone, & Gentner, 1993), on the one hand, but also phenomena such as colour spreading and transparency as well as the after-effects of colour, size, shape, orientation, depth and motion, on the other hand. But the basic question still remains: Are there general comparative, i.e., cross-species rules of how perceptual ("experiential") phenomena are related to brain functions (DeWeerd & Pessoa, 2003; Dresp, 1997; Peterhans & von der Heydt, 1986; Spillmann & Dresp, 1995; Teller, 1984; von der Heydt & Peterhans, 1989; for other accounts see Costall, Sinico, & Palmer, 2003; Parovel, 2003; Uttal, 1995, 1998)? After all, most of what we know so far about the underlying brain processes arises from a very small, selected group of non-human animals (see Dewsbury, 1989, 1992; Parker, 2002; Riley & Langley, 1993).

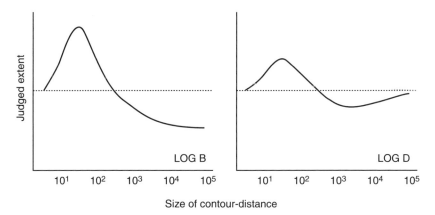

Figure 1.5 Predictions derived from a mathematical contour-distance model of relative size contrast in the Ebbinghaus-Titchener illusion. The two predictive trends represent over-estimation versus under-estimation (assimilation vs. contrast) of focal circle size (*X*) as dependent on the background context (*C*). *Left*: contour-context prediction with variable background (*B*) and distance (*D*) at zero (*D* = 0). *Right*: distance-context prediction with constant *B* and variable distance (*D* < *X*); (see also chapter 2, pp. 25–27). (Adapted from Sarris, 1986.)

The evolutionary perspective on comparative perception

An illuminating example for the relational and absolute aspects of comparative psychophysics is provided by the research on music perception and octave generalization in monkeys as compared with that of human infants. For instance, it has been experimentally shown that rhesus monkeys perform complete octave generalization to human childhood songs and tonal melodies. In other words, they behave in line with *music gestalts* since the tonal melodies during training are transposed to test melodies, over two octaves, in the sense of relational – but sometimes also absolute – perceptual memory (Hulse, Takeuchi, & Braaten, 1992; Wright, Rivera, Hulse, Shyan, & Neiworth, 2000; for findings with human infants see Trehub, 1990, 1993, 2003; Trehub & Trainor, 1994). Note that such basic transposition facts also imply the assumption of a rudimentary *number* ("numerosity") system in human infants and animals (see Dehaene, 1997; Emmerton, 2001; Emmerton & Delius, 1993; furthermore see chapter 6).

A note on the evolutionary perspective

It must be noted that the – highly scattered – literature contains typical criticisms raised against some limited perspectives in comparative psychology (e.g., Riley & Langley, 1993; see here Table 1.1). A useful introductory text on instinct, environment, and behaviour has been provided by Lea (1984)

Table 1.1 Some major criticisms raised against limited perspectives of mainstream comparative psychology (see Table 1.2). (Adapted from Riley & Langley, 1993.)

Criticism	Example
Preoccupation with instrumentation	Research of technique rather than the comparative analysis of behaviour
Artificial laboratory environment	Lacking concern for the natural environment of the animal species under study
Small portion of behaviourally relevant aspects	Exclusion of the wide range of potentially interesting behaviour
Limited range of the species chosen	Studying only monkeys, cats, or pigeons
Lack of evolutionary impacts	Neglecting the study of phylogenetic as well as ontogenetic changes in behaviour

and it deals, for instance, with such questions like: What can the evolution of animal behaviour tell us about human behaviour? More specifically, how good an account of animal behaviour can we give in terms of evolution, and how do humans fit in with or deviate from the pattern established for other animals?

At any rate, the study of both the similarities and differences of the various animal species might be seen in light of the classic evolutionary and behavioural research promoted many years ago by Jakob von Uexküll (1934/1957), Mathilde Hertz (1933, 1934; see Kressley-Mba, 2001; Kressley-Mba & Jäger, 2003), and Konrad Lorenz (1935, 1958). This broad topic, among other things, also asserts the high significance of the general species-specific context, i.e., *environmental context* (for the history of the concept of evolution see Gould, 2002; Lea, 1984; see also Corballis, 2003; Sell, Hagen, Cosmides, & Tooby, 2003).

The more recent work of Gilbert Gottlieb (e.g., 1998, 2002; Gottlieb & Krasnegor, 1985) and Robert B. Lickliter has corroborated the relevance of an evolutionary research methodology (Lickliter & Bahrick, 2000; Lickliter, Bahrick, & Honeycutt, 2002; see also Table 1.2). A somewhat representative account of the respective potentials of cognitive ethology in comparative psychology has been documented in a recent collection of seminal papers (Bekoff, Allen, & Burkhardt, 2002). However, no systematic psychophysics approach, in making the otherwise important accomplishments of modern ethology and comparative psychology more precise, has been offered until today (see chapter 3).

Using the major findings of his comparative works with pigeons, monkeys and apes, Anthony A. Wright made the point that birds, monkeys and humans show impressive qualitative similarities in such highly complex cognitive tasks as abstract concept memory, and that they differ only in quantitative terms. In making this claim he cites Papini's (2002) review, which concludes that learning phenomena in general are very stable across a wide

Table 1.2 Typical differences between comparative-developmental evolutionary psychology and cognitive psychology. (Adapted from Parker, 2002.)

	Comparative-developmental and "evolutionary" psychology	Cognitive ethology
Disciplinary origins	Comparative psychology, animal behaviour, developmental psychology	Comparative psychology, ethology/animal behaviour, cognitive psychology
Key concepts	Species-specific developmental stages, adaptation	Species-specific learning, consciousness, perceptual cognitive adaptation
Topics	Developmental stages in physical knowledge, logical and symbolic knowledge, self-awareness	Communication, intentionality, self-awareness, cognitive maps, number encoding
Methodologies	Observation, cross-fostering experiments	Observation in wild, model testing
Taxa	Closely related species: e.g., great apes (in-group) in contrast to monkeys (out-group)	Distantly related model species of birds and mammals: e.g., pigeons, monkeys, bats, rats
Goals	Identifying similarities and differences among primates: reconstructing the evolution of cognitive development	Identifying species-specific learning abilities; discovering adaptive significance of abilities

variety of animal species (Wright et al., 2000; Wright, Rivera, Katz, & Bachevalier, 2003). This book deals only briefly with the issues of these still undecided – hotly debated – implications (see chapter 6). It suffices here to state that most animal psychophysical tasks as described in this book have afforded much simpler perceptual-cognitive capacities than those used in Wright's and other investigators' research.

Summary and conclusions

In this chapter on the epistemology of relational perception and psychophysics some fundamental issues of present-day comparative perception and psychophysics have been outlined (or, at least touched) including tentatively a developmental-evolutionary perspective of modern research.

It should be emphasized, most of all, that beyond the classical issue of sensation this book deals mainly with the problem of perceptual-cognitive relativity in psychophysics. The major, still unsolved, question has been raised here as follows: *Are there viable bridges between the modern quantitative approaches of gestalt psychology and perceptual-cognitive psychophysics?*

The two basic implications of this fundamental question are the following: In light of the explanatory gaps (as illustrated in Figure 1.1), a liberal and constructive standpoint of systematic comparative experimentation is suggested (see Shepard, 2001). Furthermore, this question – how to overcome the epistemological gaps – is addressed by a comparative psychophysical approach and treated here in a step-by-step sequence in the following chapters (2–6).

2 Frame-of-reference models in psychophysics

> I cannot help noting that there has always been a preference for peripheralistic explanations in terms of sensory mechanisms over more central ones in the history of the field of perception ... A similar fate has befallen the concept of *framework* in its application to the phenomenon of induced motion.
>
> (Rock, 1990, p. 247)

Introduction

Suppose that Peter Pim is in his jet plane from Los Angeles to New York and he is asked during his trip what time it is. If he were giving his answer precisely, Peter would not only read his watch but provide a time judgement related either to Los Angeles and/or New York time. Without doubt, clock time depends on his spatial time "frame of reference". In this book, however, the frame-of-reference concept has a different, more special meaning (see chapter 1, pp. 8–9, see also Baird, 1970; Yonas, 2003).

The frame-of-reference concept

The term frame of reference (FR), originally stemming from gestalt psychology, is understood here to denote a key concept that has something to do with the perception of the stimulus relations that form the basis of most, if not all, of the so-called "contextual" effects in perception and psychophysics. Note that the psychological meaning of the FR term varies across fields of research such as perception, psychophysics, cognition, and even social psychology, which may sometimes be confusing. Also within the field of perception and psychophysics the FR term has different meanings (Sarris, 1975, 2004; see also Rock, 1990). A purely context-free perceptual situation – in its literal sense – is experimentally provided in a so-called *Ganzfeld* (e.g., Avant, 1965; Haber & Hershenson, 1973, Figure 8.1, p. 178; Metzger, 1929).

Basic problems in psychophysics

Some major issues in psychophysics are easily recognized by considering the logic of Ernst H. Weber's (1834) and Gustav T. Fechner's (1860) most influential contributions to psychology (Weber's law and Fechner's law). Note that Fechner tried to develop a quantitative law based on Weber's experimental data which predicts precisely the thresholds for any given sensory modality; namely any just noticeable difference (Δ S) was said to be a constant ratio to its basic reference stimulus S_o – in other words, Δ S/S_o = constant. Whereas Weber's law is valid at best only within narrow experimental limits, it is clear that Fechner's law, which rests mathematically on Weber's data, is also severely limited (e.g., see Baird, 1997). In the present context it is worth noting that Weber's law constitutes a basic principle of sensory *relativity* – after all, it states that the numerical value of any just noticeable difference is not constant but variable relative to the magnitude of its respective reference stimulus S_o. Strangely enough, this basic fact of psychophysical relativity has hardly been acknowledged and extended in modern research (see Boring, 1942; Murray, 1993).

The important influences of the omnipresent "context" have been recognized in the more recent psychophysics research (e.g., Gescheider, 1988). For instance, Norman H. Anderson (e.g., 1983, 2001) has proposed a general context-effect model (see Table 2.1 and Figure 2.1). In contrast to the traditional postulate of sensory psychophysics relying more or less on the assumption of context-free subjective measurements, the present approach has started with the basic idea of a complex perceptual-cognitive processing in a given *context-dependent* psychophysical setting (Figure 2.1; see Sarris, 1975, 2004; see also Lockhead, 1992, 2004).

Perceptual-cognitive judgements

For many years there existed, not only in the realm of psychophysics, two contrasting approaches in perceptual research, namely the sensory-neurophysiological research tradition as opposed to a more perceptual-cognitive approach (see Baird, 1997; Kaernbach et al., 2004; Laming, 1997; Sarris, 2004, 2006). A critical state-of-the-art article by Daniel A. Weintraub

Table 2.1 Some basic issues in psychophysics ("invalidity", "noise", "bias"). Whereas these three major psychophysical problems are usually confounded, the "contextual" effects on comparative psychophysical judgements are of primary interest here. (Adapted from Sarris, 2004.)

	Three major problems in psychophysics
Measurement devices	Problem of scale convergence ("*invalidity*")
Instrumental precision	Problem of inter- and intra-individual variability ("*noise*")
Contextual effects	Problem of scale distortion ("*bias*")

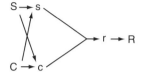

Figure 2.1 Focal (*S, s*) and context (*C, c*) stimuli, according to a general psychophysics model of perceptual information-integration (Anderson,
1983, 2001). The symbols *S* and *C* represent the explicit stimulus
properties whereas *s* and *c* mean implicit, i.e., nonobservable representations; *r* means the integrated implicit, *R* the explicit response
variable. The implicit responses are assumed either at an "early"
(bottom-up) or "late" (top-down) stage of information processing.
(Adapted from Bredenkamp & Sarris, 1987.)

– published already in 1975, in the *Annual Review of Psychology* – contains an
amusing description of a confrontation of these opposing research strategies
in sensation and perception:

> Two large tribes . . . neurophysiological theorists and psychological-
> process theorists . . . The former deal in flesh and blood mechanisms
> (e.g. neural lateral interactions), the latter in descriptive labels for psycho-
> logical functions . . . There's a jungle down there, trails that lead nowhere,
> overgrown with tangled roots, vegetation that is perpetually green but
> never flowers, and these unfriendly tribes separated by nearly impene-
> trable forest. The tribes skirmish only occasionally because they seldom
> venture from their own clearings, which they stand ready to defend at a
> moment's notice . . . The tribes can be distinguished by language, habits
> and lifestyle.
>
> (Weintraub, 1975, p. 263)

Until today different camps in psychophysics relied more or less heavily
on the following traditional misconceptions ("myths") as to the role of
contextual effects in psychophysics:

- *Myth 1:* "Context effects" in psychophysics are very special, unimportant
  side-effects, which only a few researchers have demonstrated to exist.
  Wrong!
- *Myth 2:* The nature of the "contextual" effects in psychophysics is easy to
  study experimentally, in both humans and animals. *Wrong again!*

- *Myth 3:* A simple, one-stage process model may fully account for most, if not all, psychophysical context effects. *Still wrong!*

Nowadays, the more perceptual-cognitive perspective is preferred mainly by those scientists who emphasize the importance of the contextual perceptual processing in psychophysics, i.e., stimulus-related context effectiveness, referred to here as the *stimulus context*. The following quotation illustrates Wendell R. Garner's (1954) classic finding of dramatic context effects in a loudness-estimation task:

> [The participants'] judgments depended on the immediate context rather than on the loudness of the stimulus. [Typically] . . . in experiments on the estimation of sensations the influence of context is very powerful and the accuracy of judgment is . . . poorer by one to two orders revealed in the measurement of just noticeable differences.
>
> (Laming, 1986, p. 657; quoted after Sarris, 2004)

In addition to context effects on scaling, there are still several other unsolved issues to be considered, but not treated in length here (see Table 2.1; see also Baird, 1997; Hellström, 1985; Laming, 1997; Lockhead, 1992, 2004; Poulton, 1989; Teghtsoonian & Teghtsoonian, 1971, 1997, 2003; West, Ward, & Khosia, 2000).

Relational psychophysics and frame-of-reference effects

Whereas classical sensory psychology relied mainly on the assumption of absolute, i.e., invariant stimulus-response laws, the relation theory in psychophysics is based on the general premise that, in principle, one and the same stimulus may be perceived and judged very differently as a function of the variables implied by the total contextual situation at hand (see Figure 2.1). For instance, the psychophysical scale values for pitch are strongly dependent on the respective stimulus range provided by the physical inputs. Thus, the slope of the stimulus-response curves varies inversely with the size of the stimulus range. This well-established – but in classical psychophysics not well-appreciated – fact is illustrated here by a graphical representation of the findings taken from Sarris's psychophysical work (Figure 2.2; see Sarris, 1976, 2004; see also Marks & Algom's review, 1998).

On the role of context effects

Many researchers, including Namba and Kuwano (2000) have discussed the validity of scaling in relation to frame-of-reference effects in psychophysics; and they suggest a general convergent-operation research strategy (see also Anderson, 1975; Birnbaum, 1974; Mellers & Birnbaum, 1982; Sarris & Haider, 1970). Note that nowadays the relevance of context effects in

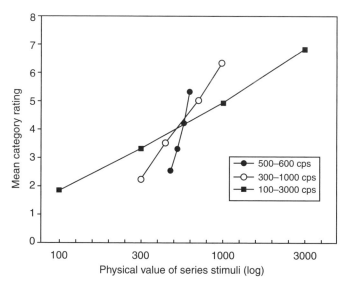

Figure 2.2 Range effects in psychophysics, with three different pitch-stimulus series (500–600 cps, 300–1000 cps, 100–3000 cps). The category ratings are strongly dependent on the respective stimulus range provided by the physical inputs of the three pitch series. Thus the slope (steepness) of the three stimulus-response curves varies inversely with the size of the stimulus range (in case of no-context effects the experimental trends would follow one and the same line = zero slope). (Adapted from Sarris, 1976, 2004.)

psychophysics has become more than ever a hotly debated topic (see, for instance, the recent discussions on such effects at the international conferences of psychophysics in Larnaka/Cyprus (Berglund & Borg, 2003) and Coimbra/Portugal (Oliveira, Teixeira, Borges, & Ferro, 2004). In general, the following facts are important in present-day psychophysics. The major types of contextual "shifts" of psychophysical scale values are due to the stimulus *range* (see Figure 2.2), stimulus *asymmetry* ("anchoring"), and stimulus *frequency* variations (see Figure 3.2; see also Laming, 1997; Marks & Algom, 1998; Poulton, 1989). Their theoretical relevance was ignored if not bluntly denied by S. Smith Stevens and his followers: i.e., such effects were essentially downgraded as secondary or irrelevant "biases" of the assumed true psychophysical values (e.g., Stevens, 1958, 1975). An attempt to deal with context effects systematically called for a new axiomatic approach, namely a relational measurement theory in psychophysics (Krantz, 1972; Shepard, 1974, 1978, 1981a, 1981b, 2001; see also Luce, 2004).

During the last years there has been published an enormous amount of work on human – but not animal – context effects in psychophysics (see the overviews by Baird, 1997; Laming, 1997; Marks & Algom, 1998). In the following section, only three typical FR models are described, namely

Harry Helson's (1947, 1964) *adaptation-level (AL)* theory, Allen Parducci's (1965, 1983, 1995) *range-frequency* approach, and this author's *similarity-classification* model (Sarris, 1971/1975, 1994, 2004).

Adaptation-level model: a sensory-perceptual concept

The adaptation level (AL) is the central concept of Helson's context-effect theory in psychophysics. According to this approach, the AL is conceived as a so-called neutral stimulus, which elicits psychological zero responses (e.g., neither "soft" nor "loud"). It has been assumed to function as a point of reference for all the other stimuli to be perceived and judged. In this theory the relational character of psychophysical ratings is expressed by the following mathematical equation:

$$R = F(Si/AL), \tag{2.1}$$

where R refers to the rating-scale response made for a given test stimulus Si, and AL is that stimulus which elicits a neutral behavioural or perceptual response. The symbol F signifies a general mathematical log function. The AL results from the interaction of three classes of stimuli: namely (1) the focal stimuli (Si), which are in the centre of attention; (2) the background stimuli, in Helson's experiments called "anchor" or "contextual" stimuli (C); (3) the residual stimuli, i.e., those stimuli which arise from previous experience (E) and which produce various unspecified effects. Thus, the following relation holds for the AL terms:

$$AL = \bar{S}^a_{\,tot}\, C^b\, E^c. \tag{2.2}$$

The series or test stimuli enter into this relation as a geometrical mean, while the exponents a, b and c represent relative "weighting" constants which are to be empirically established ($a+b+c = 1$).

Because Helson omits the manipulation of past experience in his research paradigm, for practical purposes Equation (2.2) should be rewritten as:

$$R = F[Si/(\bar{S}^g_{\,tot}\, C^{(1-g)})], \tag{2.3}$$

where g and $(1 - g)$ are the new – constant – relative weighting factors adding up to 1. This multiplicative model predicts *monotonic* trends for context effects, namely psychophysical contrast effects, whereby each judgement is determined by the *ratio* of a given series stimulus to the AL.

Remarks

The basic assumption of a simple monotonic relationship between the variable context (anchor) stimulus and the quantity of the psychophysical contrast effects does not hold empirically. In reality, the experimental trend in question tends to be cubic, i.e., *tritonic* in nature (see below). This fundamental fact means:

- At best, the AL model's main prediction holds only in the middle region of a given psychophysical dimension.
- The AL theory rests on an ill-conceived assumption of the *sensory* nature of all psychophysical judgements. Instead, the conception of perceptual-cognitive stimulus classification is more appropriate in many if not most cases.
- Helson's postulate of the adaptation level representing a psychological zero point (internal referent) has not been supported and is therefore refuted (e.g., Parducci, 1965, 1982, 1983; Sarris, 1967, 1971/1975, 2004).

On the other hand, Helson's AL model has been fruitful in a few subfields of perceptual research, at least as a conceptual rule of thumb. Accordingly, this approach continues to be of at least some heuristic interest (Marks & Algom, 1998; Thomas, 1993; see also Gilchrist, 1990, 1994; Gilchrist & Bonato, 1995).

Range-frequency model: a perceptual-judgement model

According to Parducci's (1965, 1982, 1983, 1995) range-frequency (RF) model psychophysical ratings result as a compromise between two perceptual-cognitive tendencies, namely: (a) the tendency to divide the range up into equal sections ("subranges"); (b) the tendency to assign the same frequency (number) of stimuli to each category. This means that in the course of the presentation series the judgemental scale changes as a function of the stimulus range, on the one hand, and of the stimulus-frequency distribution, on the other. Thus the average judgement for a given stimulus Si ensues according to the following prediction:

$$R_{SiD} = mR_{iD} + (1 - m)F_{iD}, \tag{2.4}$$

where m means a constant weighting factor ($0 < m < 1$), and F_{iD} is the frequency value of Si of the stimulus-frequency distribution D. Under the special consideration of having calculated the subjective values R_{iD} and F_{iD}, the judgemental behaviour R_{Si} for a given stimulus Si is predicted by an extension of Equation (2.4a) as follows:

$$R_{Si} = m(S_i - S_{min})/(S_{max} - S_{min}) + (1 - m)(r_i - 1)/(N - 1), \tag{2.4a}$$

where m means the above-mentioned weighting factor, S_{min} the lower-end stimulus, S_{max} the upper-end stimulus of a given series, r the rank of Si, in the given contextual set, and N the rank of the highest stimulus.

Remarks

Parducci's RF approach rests on the assumption of *perceptual-cognitive* classification in psychophysics (see also Sander, 1998; Sarris & Parducci, 1978; Sarris & Sander, 1997; Sokolov, Pavlova, & Ehrenstein, 2000; see also Ward, 1973, 1979, 1987, 1990, 1992, 2003). Contrary to AL theory, the RF model correctly predicts higher overall means judgements for periodically ascending rather than for periodically descending series.

Also in contrast to the AL paradigm, Parducci proceeds without introducing special "background" and/or "residual" stimuli. Typically, the series' range as well as the frequency distribution of the series stimuli are varied systematically. The effects of variation of stimulus distribution may be interpreted either in terms of contrast effects, or in terms of psychophysical memory processes – for instance: If "large" stimuli are more frequently presented than "small" ones, then the presentation of a large stimulus will lead to an under-estimation, and vice versa (perceptual-cognitive "contrast"). However, a similar result is to be expected if the subject adapts the category scale to the frequency and range of the stimulus series increasingly better over time (see also Petrov & Anderson, 2005; Stewart & Brown, 2004).

During the last few years several refinements of Parducci's RF model have been suggested; for instance, by Douglas H. Wedell, USA, for the stimulus-discrimination case with either the two-, three-, or nine-category rating scale (Wedell, 1985, 1996, 2004), and by Gert Haubensak and Peter Petzold, Germany, for the role of short- and long-term memory in the frame-of-reference processing with category ratings (e.g., Haubensak, 1992; Haubensak & Petzold, 2002; Petzold & Haubensak, 2004). It should be noted that the RF model's basic rationale can be combined with that of other models or theories, for example with the following theory, i.e., the similarity-classification (SC) model (see below; see also Sarris & Parducci, 1978).

Similarity-classification model: a perceptual-cognitive theory

While the AL approach is oriented toward processes of sensory adaptation, this author's so-called similarity-classification (SC) model is intended as a theoretical alternative: namely, the SC model can be characterized as a perceptual-cognitive account of stimulus classification in psychophysics. In this model, the principle of perceptual classification describes and explains both the presence and absence of context effects, and also the diminishing effects of the psychophysical distance (*similarity*) between the test-series stimuli and the contextual inputs.

At the same time the SC model abandons the concept of an arbitrary psychological zero point. In contrast to the AL model, the "point of subjective indifference" (PSI) is regarded solely as a convenient psychometric value which must not be taken as the standard for judgement. The quantitative SC model for *individual* stimuli represents judgemental behaviour as a function of the series stimulus *Si* and of the contextual stimuli *C*, whereas the subject-ive similarity between *C* and *Si* is introduced as a variable weighting parameter *w* and (*w*+1) for *C* and S_i respectively:

$$R = Si^{(1+w)}/C^w,\tag{2.5}$$

where $w_{c \geq s} = 1/(1+C/Si)$, and $w_{c < s} = 1/(1+Si/C)$.

The mass of experimental data for many psychophysical dimensions (e.g., pitch, line, lifted weights) largely support the SC model (see example below, pp. 27–29).

Remarks

This non-additive Equation (2.5) predicts nonmonotonic – i.e., tritonic (cubic) – trends for psychophysical contrast effects: namely, small distances between the contextual stimulus *C* and the series stimulus *Si* lead to relatively strong psychophysical contrast effects (see the maxima/minima of the trend curves in Figure 2.3, p. 28), while large distances lead to a gradual disappear-ance of these effects (*asymptotes* of the tritonic curves) – the so-called *Sarris effect* (Link, 2004; Parducci, 2004).

   Note that the original SC model predicts only the usual psychophysical contrast effects, but not the less well-known assimilation phenomenon (how-ever, cf. Figure 1.5, p. 12; for some recent mathematical models of psycho-physical "assimilation" see Petrov & Anderson, 2004; see also DeCarlo, 1994, 2003; DeCarlo & Cross, 1990).

The SC model and its application

A few studies on optico-geometric distortions (OGD) have extended the scope of the SC model (the *Sarris effect*: see Link, 2004; Parducci, 2004). As an important example take Frank Restle's (1978; personal communication, 2 February 1976) special account. Restle's studies have been conducted on illusion figures: for instance, a test line on shaft with square boxes at each end (*Baldwin figure*; see Figure 1.4). Restle and Merryman (1968, 1969) found that judgements of line length *decreased* with box size. The work used very small boxes as well as large ones and showed two facts: (a) the line *with* boxes was judged longer than a control line without boxes (i.e., assimilation, not contrast); (b) when boxes were quite small (having a diameter less than a quarter the length of the test line) the judgement of line length actually *increased* with box size.

SC theory and Restle's application

In particular, the SC theory was employed by Restle (1978) in the follow-ing form. First, the model of judgements of length of a line of length X, surrounded by boxes of width B and in a field of (unknown) size K, was used as follows:

$$J(X) = X/A, \tag{2.6}$$

where

$$A = B^W_B K^W_{K]}{}^{J/W}_B{}^{+W}_K. \tag{2.7}$$

Here the SC theory was introduced by saying that if $B<X$, $W_B = f(B/X)$. We do not know the function f except for this: When the box is of *zero* magnitude it does not exist, and therefore its weight must be zero: $f(0) = 0$.

As an example to calculate, we set (for $B<X$):

$$W_B = \beta B, \tag{2.8}$$

where β is a positive constant.

Second, another fact may be used (see Restle, 1978, pp. 76–85). In some experiments, if the boxes are made quite large, say, $B = L$, one finds that $J_L(X)$ with this large box just equals $J_0(X)$, the judged length of that line with no box. That is, $J_L(X) = J_0(X)$ for some L. Then:

$$J_L(X) = (B_L{}^W B K^W K)^{1/W} B^+{}^W K \tag{2.9}$$

and

$$J_0(X) = K \tag{2.9a}$$

obtained from Equation (2.7) and Equation (2.8). But Equation (2.9) implies that

$$B_L = K.$$

Therefore, by locating B_L we estimate K, which always takes a large value, much larger than X or the smaller values of B. For a reasonable example, suppose the test line $X = 4$ cm. We might find that $K \approx 12$ cm. Also, if we use Equation (2.8) we estimate $\beta = .10$. Using these values, we calculate J(X) as a function of B, using this simple AL principle with the SC theory that $W(B) = \beta B$. As a result, as B increases from zero, J(X) also increases; and J(X) reaches a maximum approximately when $B = .25X$ to $B = .50X$; then as B approaches X, J(X) decreases.

Now if we let

$$W_B = \beta (^X/B),$$

when $B < X$, we find that as B increases still more, J(X) continues to decrease, but levels out eventually at the limit $W_{oo} = 0$, so $J_{oo}(X) = J_0(X)$. The experimental data have been well in line with this math model building (see the published paper by Restle, 1978; see the example below).

Note that the SC model's rationale rests mainly on the assumption of unidimensional similarity measurements. As a matter of fact, up until now it has not been extended to the multidimensional case in any strict way of mathematical and experimental analysis (however, see chapters 4 and 6; see also Gregson, 1975, 1988, 1995; Kanisza, 1994; Parovel & Vezziani, 2002). Other studies have dealt with some basic theoretical and experimental problems of perceptual learning in geometric-optical illusions under the assumption of an interaction between sensory, perceptual and cognitive-informational determinants of human and animal perception (e.g., Girgus, Coren, & Fraenkel, 1975; Sarris, 1984).

EXAMPLE

Context effects in pitch judgements

The aim of this study was to demonstrate as systematically as possible both the occurrence and disappearance of the so-called anchoring effects in pitch judgements as predicted by the SC model (Sarris, 1975, 2004).

Method

Three different pitch-stimulus series 1, 2 and 3, each consisting of five different frequencies of const. 52 Phon, were presented with a variable anchor tone. The participants (N = 520 Ss, all in all) were instructed neither to attend to nor judge the anchor stimulus. The anchor tone, which preceded each series stimulus and remained the same throughout a given experimental session, was always presented for 1 s. After a break of 1.5 s, one of the five test-series stimuli was presented for 1 s and was judged by the subjects on a 9-point *rating scale*. The values of the pitch stimuli for both the test series and the respective anchor tones were the following (anchor values in brackets):

Pitch series 1: 250, 275, 300, 325, 350 cps (25, 70, 190, 250, 310, 400, 550, 900, 3000, 10 000 cps).

Pitch series 2: 500, 525, 550, 575, 600 cps (25, 50, 70, 130, 190, 250, 400, 550, 700, 900, 1100, 1300, 3000, 7000, 10 000, 15 000 cps).

Pitch series 3: 750, 775, 800, 825, 850 cps (125, 380, 515, 630, 775, 900, 1500, 3000, 7000, 15 000 cps).

Results and discussion

The main context-pitch data, averaged separately for the three test series, followed very regular sinoidal (cubic, i.e., tritonic) trends and they reflected both the gradual occurrence and disappearance of "contextual" asymmetry-effects as predicted by the author's mathematical similarity-classification model (see Figure 2.3 for the experimental trends; for the statistical tests see Sarris, 1975). Apparently, very *extreme* ("dissimilar") context tones – relative to the given pitch series – do not influence any longer the psychophysical judgements of the focal pitch stimuli (series 1: 250–350 cps; series 2: 500–600 cps; series 3: 750–850 cps).

Intraseries context effects

In addition to these findings, some intraseries context-effect trends were experimentally obtained which are also of high theoretical significance (Figure 2.4; see also Sarris 1975, 1976). These findings illustrate again that it is important to specify the anchor effect limits for diverse stimulus ranges. The results reflect once again a basic gestalt principle in that psychologically extreme context stimuli do not belong to a given series-stimulus "class" (i.e., the *Sarris effect*). These unidimensional findings as presented here can be related to multidimensional and heteromodal anchor effect *limits* (e.g. Brown, 1953; see also Hahn, 2003; Maddox, 2002; Quinlan & Wilten, 1998). The quantitative concept of *similarity* is treated more fully elsewhere (see chapters 3 and 5).

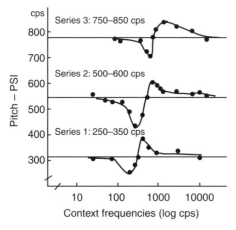

Figure 2.3 Cubic ("tritonic") trends for a systematic study of pitch context effects ("anchor" effectiveness versus context-effect limits, i.e., the *Sarris effect*). (Data from Sarris, 1975; adapted from Sarris, 2004.)

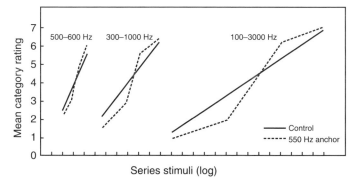

Figure 2.4 Intraseries anchor effects on pitch judgements as reflected by the ratings for the three different pitch-stimulus series as a function of the stimulus range with an intraseries anchor 550 Hertz, cps. For the abscissa values see Figure 2.3. Note that the psychologically extreme "context" stimuli for the three pitch-stimulus series (500–600 cps; 300–1000 cps; 100–3000 cps) do not exhibit psychophysical contrast effects. (Adapted from Sarris, 1976.)

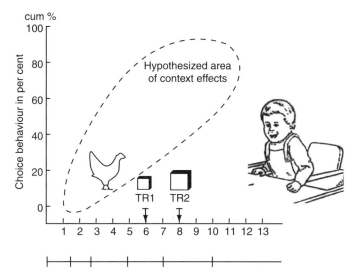

Figure 2.5 Illustration of the hypothesized spatio-temporal area of context and transposition effects on the psychophysical response in humans and animals (in contrast to G. T. Fechner's and S. S. Stevens's simple, i.e., context-free stimulus-sensation laws). (Abscissa: physical scale in arbitrary log units; ordinata: measure of relative choice behaviour in per cent; TR1, TR2: the two training stimuli; see chapter 3, Figure 3.3.) (Adapted from Sarris, 1990.)

Summary and conclusions

The influence of different perceptual-cognitive frames-of-reference constitutes a challenging problem in psychophysics (*relational psychophysics*). One
major aspect of this broad and deep issue is related to the most well-known
context effects on perceptual judgements in general and on the psychophysical
measurements in particular. Some types of unidimensional contextual shifts
arising from the stimulus-range, stimulus-asymmetry (anchoring), and
stimulus-frequency variations of test-target objects are especially noteworthy.
They deserve major attention in all areas of perception and psychophysics,
particularly because they strongly contradict the classical claim of so-called
"unbiased scales" in psychophysics. Some of the major frame-of-reference
models have been presented here, with an eye on the perceptual-cognitive
processes involved in category ratings (e.g., Sarris's SC model).

It is noteworthy that there exist quantitative as well as qualitative limits of
psychophysical context effects (see here the *Sarris effect*, p. 25), which are also
of high comparative-developmental interest, as this is shown in the next two
chapters. In this sense, Figure 2.5 illustrates the general spatio-temporal
case of hypothetical context effects – and its limits – on the psychophysical
responding in humans and other animals.

3 Behavioural psychophysics
Contrasting ideas and findings

> The tide is beginning to turn as new techniques are developed [in psychophysics] that are sensitive to context effects also in non-humans. Several researchers have now reported range effects in ... birds using quite different procedures and sensory continua ... Although it is easier to demonstrate relative stimulus encoding in humans than in animals, it is now clear that this is not an exclusively human phenomenon.
>
> (Thomas, Mood, Morrison, & Wiertelak, 1991, p. 139)

Introduction

Whereas chapter 2 dealt with three different frame-of-reference (FR) models, which rely on so-called direct methods, especially ratings and category scales, alternative psychophysical techniques are described in the following sections. These latter methods are particularly appropriate for obtaining nonverbal, namely *behavioural* data. Consider, for example, such an *indirect* method based on choice behaviour (e.g., method of pair comparison) for the study of non-linguistic or linguistically immature organisms, say, preverbal infants. An impressive illustration of auditory psychophysics in human infants was provided by Bruce A. Schneider and Sandra E. Trehub, Canada. Their psychophysical curves were based on the amount of correct head-turn (*behaviour*) as a function of varying decibel level for different test frequencies (Schneider & Trehub, 1985; Trehub, 1990, 1993, 2003; see also Cynx, 1995; Enquist & Ghirlanda, 2005; Ghirlanda, 2002; Ghirlanda & Enquist, 2003; Hulse & Cynx, 1995; Hulse, MacDougall-Shackleton, & Wisniewski, 1997).

Relevance of behavioural psychophysics

It can hardly be overstated that when entering the very heterogeneous field of comparative psychophysics one must face the interlocked conceptual problems of sensory-perceptual-cognitive processing in the preverbal human infant and also those of the non-human animal. Indeed, there are some principal epistemological questions involved when the case of information processing in animal cognition, such as *higher order perception*, is investigated.

For an illuminating example of important research in animal cognition and psychophysics consult Eric Heinemann's and Sheila Chase's, USA, work on the pigeon's cognition and memory in loudness and vision signal detection (e.g., Chase, 1983, 1997; Heinemann, 1983, 1997; see also Chase & Heinemann, 2001; Donis, Heinemann, & Chase, 1994; Heinemann & Chase, 1990; Hinson & Lockhead, 1986; Hinson & Tennison, 1998).

In general, the comparative usage of *behavioural psychophysical* methods is important for the following reasons. There has been a longstanding debate between S. S. Stevens (e.g., 1958, 1975), on the one hand, and many other psychophysicists on the other, as to the so-called linguistic ("semantic") versus perceptual relativity of psychophysical scale-value shifts (e.g., Oyama, 1959, 1977; Sarris, 1975, 1994, 2000, 2001a, 2004). This controversy led to the following main question: *How is it possible to obtain convergent-evidence also from language-free psychophysical data?* Consider these two facts:

1   In basic research of comparative psychophysics (e.g., human infant and/or animal psychophysics) the behavioural methods are the only practical techniques available (see, e.g., Wright et al., 2003 as quoted in chapter 1, p. 13f).
2   In applied settings, for example, with regard to special hearing-aid problems or for psychodiagnostic testing of cognitively impaired individuals, the choice of behavioural assessment methods is usually indicated.

Difficulties in comparative psychophysics

Concerning the research areas of human adult psychophysics (e.g., Baird, 1997), human infant psychophysics (e.g., Atkinson & Bradick, 1999; Teller, 1983, 1985, 2000) and animal psychophysics (e.g., Blake, 1999; Stebbins, 1970, 1990) there have been and still are different scientific communities engaged in the promotion and theorizing on the nature of quantitative stimulus-response relationships. Until now there was hardly any systematic exchange between the proponents of these different fields (see also chapter 2, p. 19). However, Stephen E. Palmer (2003) has recently presented some promising examples of how to overcome the barriers between verbal ("subjective") and behavioural ("objective") research methods, at least with regard to human perception. He offers several interesting illustrations of his own and other researchers' work (e.g., Kubovy & Gepshtein, 2003) in trying to bridge this gap which still exists in perceptual psychology and behavioural psychophysics.

Furthermore, following Stebbins's (1990, pp. 22–23, 1995) methodological conclusions, provided in his work on comparative psychophysics, there are some fundamental issues related to a more systematic approach in human and animal psychophysics:

•   Despite its inherent difficulties, the comparative approach in psychophysics has been and remains a dominant theme in comparative psychophysics of sensory (bottom-up) and perceptual (top-down) functioning, and it contributes increasingly to our knowledge of the evolution of human sensory and perceptual-cognitive development.

- The experimental results stemming from animal perception and psychophysics are as reliable and valid as those obtained from analogous experimentation with humans. A solid comparative research literature base continues to grow, slowly but steadily.
- The comparative work on perception and psychophysics, although highly interactive and interdisciplinary in theory and practice, has its own identity. It is characterized as being labour intensive, costly and theoretically complex.

Remarks

In this chapter, and also in chapter 4, the longstanding comparative issue of perceptual *transposition* – as a fundamental kind of relational learning (*transfer*) – is treated from a behavioural psychophysics perspective (for a modern account of the classic *Köhler-Spence-Wertheimer* debate see Pearce, 1994; Sarris, 2001b). In addition to the method of paired comparison, other behavioural methods in psychophysics, for example, the method of adjustment and the matching-to-sample method, also lead to characteristic stimulus-response relationships (e.g., Berkley & Stebbins, 1990; Stebbins, 1995). In past perception and cognition research, in contrast to sensory psychophysical work, there have been only a few comparative attempts based on behavioural-psychophysical techniques with humans as well as with animals.

A general context model of behavioural psychophysics

During the last 20 years the author's research group has developed and tested a general perceptual-cognitive psychophysics paradigm for the comparative investigation of contextual FR shifts. This behavioural paradigm, which is based on a *two-alternative two-forced choice* (*2A2FC*) method, is described below.

The psychophysical measurement of transposition

According to the author's context model of behavioural psychophysics, the *point of subjective indifference* (*PSI*, i.e., the 50 per cent rate of the two concurrent reactions) should *shift* in the direction of any given new contextual test-series centre (e.g., C1, C2), depending on the number of times the series is presented during the test phase (*post-generalization testing*; see D. M. Johnson, 1949a, 1949b; Sarris & Zoeke, 1985). More specifically, this PSI process model (see Figure 3.1), as tested with different psychophysical modalities, reads as follows:

$$PSI_{(n)} = (k\ PSI_{train} + n\ PSI_{test})/(k+n), \tag{3.1}$$

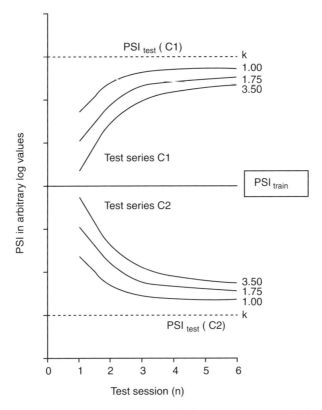

Figure 3.1 Behavioural psychophysics paradigm: graphic illustration of the PSI
process model, with its predicted functions for different k values (e.g.,
1.00, 1.75, 3.50) depending on the contextual test-series conditions
investigated (e.g., C1 and C2) and the test-session practice (n = 1, 2,
3, . . ., 6 etc.). (Adapted from Sarris, 2004.)

whereas the symbols mean:

$PSI_{(n)}$ = PSI value for the nth test trial,

PSI_{train} = PSI value of the training stimuli,

PSI_{test} = PSI value of the test series,

k = empirical weighting-factor for the given training stimuli relative to the test series, and

n = number of times the series is presented.

This general context model in behavioural psychophysics predicts asymmetric
test-series effects, but it has been also used for the handling of range and
frequency effects as well, in line with Allen Parducci's *range-frequency* model

(Figure 3.2; see also chapter 2, p. 24). Clearly, these contextual "shift" effects represent transposition behaviour (Reese, 1968; Riley, 1968), and they are perceptual-cognitive in character; but they have nothing to do with the so-called "peak shift" phenomenon of human and animal psychology (for this argument see Sarris, 1990, 2001a; Thomas, 1993).

The model's general predictions, according to Equation (3.1), imply monotonic context-effect trends. However, there are certain quantitative limits of transposition that occur with extreme test-series stimuli. For example, transposition (transfer) is observed only within the natural range of a given training- and test-stimulus dimension (see Figure 2.5). Furthermore, in line with the SC principle (see chapter 2), transposition behaviour depends not only on "distance" but also on the "similarity" properties of the perceptual stimulus under investigation.

Remarks

Note that in Equation (3.1) the empirical factor k, which expresses the relative weight due to perceptual "experience", serves as an experimental weighting factor for the given training stimuli relative to the test stimuli (see Figure 3.1). Over the years the model's implications have been tested on humans as well infrahuman subjects (see below; see also Appendix 1 for the apparatus used with chickens and Appendix 2 and Appendix 3 for some more mathematics of the psychophysics of transposition). Robert M. Gregson's book on nonlinear dynamic psychophysics has treated the transposition problem from a special nonlinear (dynamic) mathematical point of view using the author's animal psychophysical data as an illustration (Gregson, 1988, chapter 12; see here chapter 5 and Appendix 2).

In the next sections some of the basic findings for this basic behavioural psychophysics model are presented.

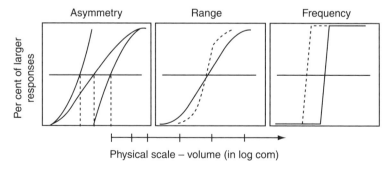

Figure 3.2 Asymmetry, range and frequency shift effects: the predicted main trends for the three major types in context psychophysics. Note that these different kinds of contextual effects as studied in a human and animal experimental set-up involve basic perceptual memory processes (see Figure 3.14). (Adapted from Sarris, 1990.)

The two-alternative two-forced choice task (2A2FC method)

In the work conducted by the author's research group, with respect to both human and animal psychophysical investigations, a successive – sometimes also simultaneous – perceptual discrimination task was used as illustrated by the following general example.

Consider two different cube sizes and discriminate them during the training stage according to the following rule: "Push the left-hand response key when the smaller of the two cubes is presented; push the right key when the cube is the larger one" (or vice versa). Next, during the test stage, the rule is: "Respond to the presentation of some additional cubes which are either smaller or larger than the training objects but use the same discrimination rule."

Figures 3.3 and 3.4 illustrate the general 2A2FC paradigm as investigated with humans and animals. If not otherwise stated, the experimental devices used in Sarris's research work were partially or fully automatic (e.g., see Appendix 1).

Human psychophysics

According to the typical experimental set-up which is graphically depicted in Figure 3.3, together with the apparatus used (Figure 3.4; Appendix 1), many

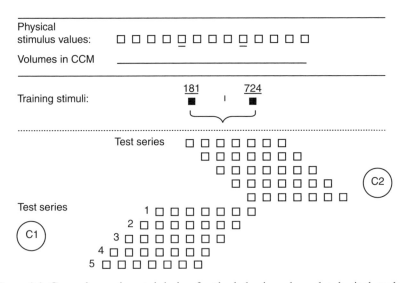

Figure 3.3 General experimental design for the behavioural-psychophysical study of contextual test effects: two training stimuli (181 ccm vs. 724 ccm) and five different sets of test series, either in the ascending C2, or descending C1, order and consisting of seven test stimuli each (physical scale, in arbitrary log units). Note that this schematic design was employed for both the human and animal psychophysics experiments. (Adapted from Sarris, 1990, 2004.)

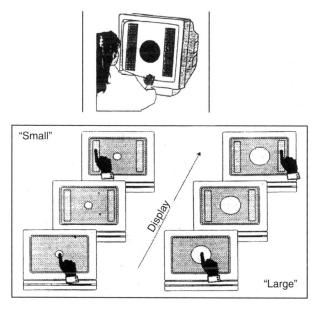

"Small"

Display

"Large"

Figure 3.4 Human psychophysics: apparatus used for preschoolers, school children, and adults for behavioural size estimation. As with all the other choice training and testing tasks provided for the younger age groups, also the size-estimation judgements were obtained in a participant-friendly game-like atmosphere (individual experimental sessions; see also Figure 4.1, p. 57).

data were gathered with human participants on the basis of the afore-mentioned behavioural-psychophysics paradigm (*size, weight, colour* and *duration* judgements). The typical empirical results stemming from *size* choices are shown here, with the psychophysical data for human adults (Table 3.1, Figure 3.5).

Each experimental data trend, established for the experimental test-context condition C1.3, C1.2, . . ., C2.2, C2.3, represents the respective contextual shift due to the six different *asymmetry* test series investigated here (the C0 trend, as a control, resulted from symmetrical testing). Clearly, all of the contextual shifts (transposition) for the different psychophysical dimensions tested are consistent with the overall prediction of lawful psychophysical "relativity" effects, due to the variable test-series asymmetry.

For instance, the ogival S-R curve depicted in Figure 3.5 for the control conditions (dotted trend C0: symmetric test condition, i.e., no test-series con-text) nicely corresponds to the classical findings in human psychophysics. In contrast, the respective left- and right-hand "shifted" curves, which are of main interest here, reflect the relative nature of psychophysical responding. In other words, one and the same psychophysical stimuli are responded to as either *large* or *small* depending on the respective context condition used. For instance, the stimulus 12 is reacted to as neither small nor large under the

Table 3.1 Shifting of test responding: the hypothetical results of *right* (R) versus *left* (L) responses for one subject (n = 1) during the generalization-test phase, for a single test session with five test blocks containing eight stimulus values (1, 2, 3, ... 7, 8). The original training stimulus values were 5 (R) and 8 (L); e.g., initially the subject responded *right* (R) to training stimulus 5 but as the test blocks progressed it showed *left* (L) responding. Note that such shift responses formed the basis for calculating the per cent of "large" responses and the PSI values, both for human and animal subjects.

				Stimulus value				
Block	*1*	*2*	*3*	*4*	*5 (R)*	*6*	*7*	*8 (L)*
1	R	R	R	R	R	R	L	L
2	R	R	R	R	R	R	L	L
3	R	R	R	L	L	L	L	L
4	R	R	L	L	L	L	L	L
5	R	R	R	L	L	L	L	L

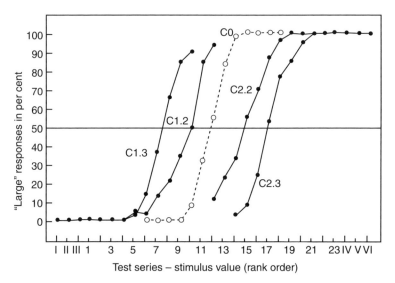

Figure 3.5 Psychophysical size-estimation data for human adults (see the age-related findings in chapter 4, Figure 4.2). The graph contains the mean context-shift results for the adult group of the human participants; main sets of experimental data trends stemming from the test phase of the size study. Each trend, C1.3, C1.2, ..., C2.2, C2.3, represents the respective contextual shifts from the different asymmetry test series investigated; the C0 trend resulted from symmetric testing. Ordinata: the per cent of large choice; abscissa: the test-series values used in rank-order units (data from Dassler & Sarris, 1997; adapted from Dassler, 2000; Sarris, 2004).

control condition, but as large under the context-test condition C1, or even as small under the condition C2.

Note that the more extreme asymmetry conditions lead to somewhat less or no context shifts. It is also notable that for each S-R curve a respective PSI measure may be easily calculated. These inferred PSI values follow the theoretical trends as depicted in Figure 3.1 for the different asymmetrical test-series conditions involved. The age-related findings for kindergarten children are presented elsewhere (chapter 4).

Using about the same size-stimulus materials, however not employing the 2A2FC technique but the *delayed matching-to-sample* method in a visual search task, Elfering (1997) found the same lawful contextual shift effects, although to a lesser degree than those obtained with the 2A2FC technique (Figure 3.6; see Elfering & Sarris, 2005). The following example

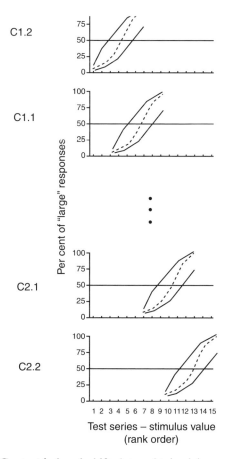

Figure 3.6 Context-induced shift data, obtained in a visual search task with human participants on the basis of the delayed matching-to-sample method: convergent size-estimation findings (schematic graph). (Adapted from Elfering, 1997; Elfering & Sarris, 2005.)

illustrates parts of the author's unidimensional studies in context (relational) psychophysics, in this case *time estimation*.

EXAMPLE

Human psychophysics: Time estimation (2A2FC)

The question under which condition *time-perception* judgements will be shown to be context dependent, namely relative, has also been investigated by the author's research group, again by implementation of a post discrimination-generalization procedure, whereby the asymmetry of a given test-stimulus series was systematically varied (Cangöz, 1999; see also Wearden & Ferrara, 2004). In these time-estimation studies it was shown once again that the point of subjective indifference (PSI), the measure of central tendency, shifted during the test phase from the training PSI towards the centre of the respective test series. These context-dependent effects were predicted according to the author's "*integrative stimulus-generalization*" model as described above (p. 33; see Weser, Arlt, & Sarris, 2000).

Method

Participants

A total of $N = 58$ students served as participants, mostly psychology undergraduates from the University of Frankfurt. They were trained and tested in individual experimental sessions.

Stimulus materials and apparatus

The stimuli consisted of seven different durations varying in equal log-unit steps, i.e. 1.3, 1.8, 2.5, 3.3, 4.5, 6.0, 8.1 seconds. They were used to construct two pairs of training stimuli along with three descending and ascending overlapping test series, each containing five different durations. Altogether during the test stage, seven time-duration stimuli were presented on a monitor as a comparative circle with variable lengths of time.

During training the participant, who was seated in front of the computer screen, was told to press two different keyboard buttons, either the left one for an apparently "short" or the right one for a seemingly "long" duration (and vice versa). The training-performance criterion was set at 18 correct out of 20 choices for the alternative category-choice method. Note that the experimenter's feedback was provided only during the training phase but never during the testing stages C2.1, C2.2, C2.3 (ascending order) and C1.3, C1.2, C1.1 (descending order).

Results and discussion

The main results obtained for the three different category-choice conditions, both under the descending (C1) and the ascending (C2) test-series conditions have been described and discussed elsewhere (Weser et al., 2000). Again, the experimental PSI trends followed either the downward or the upward shifting direction as predicted from the model. Data inspection showed no systematic differences between the experimental trends gained for the different category-number conditions. In other words, under the conditions used it does not matter how many response alternatives are provided during the testing phase (see, however, Hofer, 1988; see also Chase, 1983; Sander, 1998; Sander & Sarris, 1997).

Further work with durations consisting of milliseconds instead of seconds, such as the use of extremely brief training (c. 75–200 ms) and test-series (25–500 ms) stimuli, led to very similar context-dependent shifts – thus extending our findings considerably (Figure 3.7; see Sarris & Schnehage-Poci, 2004; Schnehage-Poci & Sarris, 2004). Recent overviews of time perception are provided elsewhere (e.g., Church, 2003; Fraisse, 1984; Grondin, 2001; see also Jones & Wearden, 2004; Richelle & Lejeune, 1990).

The role of memory in behavioural psychophysics

This behavioural-psychophysics paradigm, together with the author's behavioural PSI model, has been successfully tested in human psychophysics

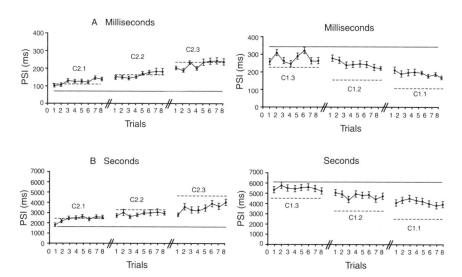

Figure 3.7 Psychophysical time-estimation PSI data, obtained under different context conditions. A milliseconds; B seconds of the time-duration stimuli. (Adapted from Sarris & Schnehage-Poci, 2004; Schnehage-Poci & Sarris, 2004.)

with the use of different choice-behaviour tasks for lifted weights, sizes, colours, and durations (for animal data see the next section; see also chapter 4 for the developmental case). This approach in psychophysics is also related to the *memory* ("mnestic") processes involved. After all, it is based on an integration of discrimination training and stimulus-generalization testing (transposition), on the one hand, and psychophysical stimulus-context variations on the other (see also Balsam & Tomie, 1985; Berkley & Stebbins, 1990; Blough, 2001). Typically, the important factor of experience (e.g., perceptual "practice" with the psychophysical stimuli used) was largely ignored in earlier psychophysical research.

Remarks

Until recently the choice behaviour for a given stimulus was predicted solely as a function of the situational contextual conditions (e.g., training or control series vs. range, anchor stimuli, frequency distribution, and so on). However, combining the SC model (see Equation 2.5) with a stimulus-generalization approach, a simple process model (see Equation 3.1) results which implies that human and animal subjects change their choice behaviour depending, first, on the situational context conditions (i.e., the *relations* of training stimuli to test stimuli) but also, second, on the amount of previous experience with the various test stimuli (Figure 3.2; see below the section "Memory and Perceptual Processes"; see also chapter 5).

At this point it should be noted that multidimensional context effects in human psychophysics follow quite different perceptual-cognitive rules (Figure 3.8). For the sake of simplicity, they are presented and discussed elsewhere (see chapter 4, pp. 59–62).

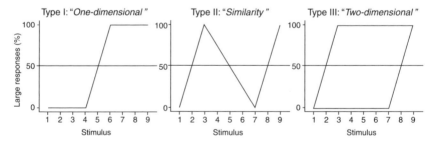

Figure 3.8 Multidimensional psychophysics (two-dimensional case): the three predicted types of behavioural choice responses (Type I, Type II, Type III), namely: judgements based on only one dimension (Type I), judgements based on the similarity between training and test stimuli (Type II), and judgements based on both dimensions (Type III). (Adapted from Hauf & Sarris, 2001a, 2001b.)

Animal psychophysics

Relevant background literature on the bird's visual perception and cognition has been presented in the overview books by Andrew (1991), Rogers (1995) and Zeigler and Bischof (1993). One of the main arguments in favour of Sarris's research group's behavioural psychophysics approach stems from the comparative investigations with non-human subjects, namely domestic chickens (*Gallus gallus domesticus*; see Figure 3.9). In a series of experiments conducted with different groups of chickens, a choice-discrimination procedure was used along with a post-discrimination generalization procedure analogous to the human psychophysics experiments, which contained the variable

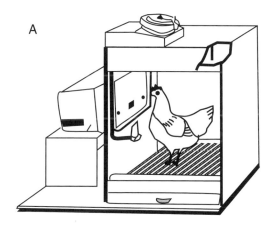

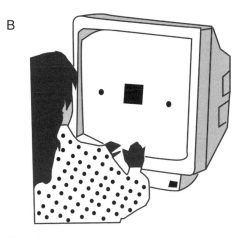

Figure 3.9 Apparatus used in comparative psychophysics (see Figure 3.3): A Animal psychophysics (see Appendix 1); B human psychophysics (see Table 3.1).

"contextual" test series under study. For instance, the variable volume of different-sized cubes served as the physical continuum, during both the training and the testing phase (see the *example* below).

Especially for the investigation of animals in past research it was difficult, if not impossible, to clearly demonstrate contextual effects if an inappropriate training and testing methodology had been employed (see the respective notes by Thomas, 1993; Thomas et al., 1991).

EXAMPLE

Animal psychophysics: Unidimensional size estimation (2A2FC)

This experiment with chickens examined the question of the gradual occurrence and disappearance of contextual effects in the chicken's psychophysical response when using the generalization-testing procedure, analogous to that employed in human psychophysics (Sarris, 1990, 1994).

Method

Six chickens (*hubbards*), approximately seven weeks old at the beginning of the investigation, served as subjects (see Appendix 1). Food was withheld for 18 hours prior to the daily training or test session. Water was continuously available in the home cage. The chickens were kept in individual cages but were allowed to move freely in groups in a scratching pen for at least two hours after their daily session. A computer-controlled apparatus permitted the successive presentation of three-dimensional cubes. These objects were automatically presented, one by one, in front of a wall on which two pecking keys were mounted, one to the left and one to the right of the stimulus object. The cubes were located on different plates along a wheel. For each trial a motor turned the wheel to the correct position from which the plate with the appropriate object was hydraulically lifted into the opening at the floor of the box.

Stimulus materials and procedure

The stimuli were red cubes consisting of equal geometric steps but differing in volume. Each subject was trained with the same pair of training stimuli – namely a 215 cc and a 608 cc cube – but tested with three different test-stimulus series (seven cubes, each). For the small contextual series, C1, the geometric mean of the training-stimulus values was the largest of the test object; for the large contextual series, C2, it was the smallest of the test objects. A null-test series, C0, was provided as the experimental control condition. For each chicken the experiment consisted of three phases: (a) key training (preliminary phase); (b) successive discrimination training; (c) generalization testing (shifting).

After preliminary training, each chicken was trained to discriminate between the two training stimuli according to the rule: "*Go left and peck at the left key when the smaller of the two cubes is presented; go right and peck at the right key when the cube is the larger one.*" This left-right rule was fully balanced for the six chickens during training and testing. Daily training sessions consisted of 50 trials. The sequence of the training-stimulus pairs was randomized with the restriction that each stimulus was presented equally often. A correct behavioural choice (i.e., the chicken pecked the correct key) was reinforced by allowing access to the respective food magazine for 3 seconds. An incorrect key choice was immediately followed by darkness, and the same stimulus was presented again after 6 seconds (correction trial). After reaching the learning criterion of at least 95 per cent correct choices for three successive training sessions, the six chickens were randomly assigned to one of three test conditions C0, C1, and C2. Each test series was presented six times daily during the six test sessions. Differential reinforcement was no longer provided (i.e., all test-series choices were positively reinforced).

Results and discussion

The average number of training days required for reaching the learning criterion was 45. Figure 3.10 shows the changes in the obtained mean S-R functions over the three test stages, whereby the percentage of large responses defines the behavioural measure. The data of two daily test sessions, comprised of the total number of 12 responses for each of the seven different test stimuli, were combined to form the test stages 1, 2 and 3. The three graphs, in the figure from left to right (Figure 3.10), show the psychophysical functions undergoing systematic response changes under the two different asymmetric test conditions, C1 and C2 (shifts = transposition).

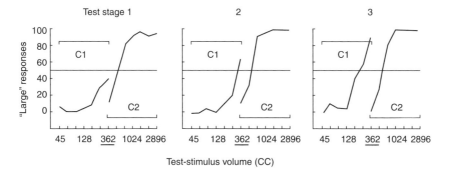

Figure 3.10 Gradual occurrence of context-dependent size-response trends for chickens during the post-discrimination test stages 1, 2 and 3. Note that the contextual shifts developed only gradually from stage 1 through 3 as predicted by the model Equation 6. (Adapted from Sarris, 1990, 1994.)

As predicted by the FR model, the two chickens tested with the small context series, C1, used very few large responses in the beginning, while the other two animals tested with the large series, C2, used many large choices (stage 1). Note in particular that the large reaction rate progressively decreased over the test stages (stages 2 and 3). In other words, one and the same test stimuli were increasingly judged either as large or small depending on the test series used. As a consequence, the PSI shifted towards the centre of the test series, C1 or C2, respectively. For example, the middle-sized stimulus, the 362 cc cube which was physically equal for all test series, was responded to as large on approximately 50 per cent of the trials only at the beginning of the testing phase (stage 1): The percentage of these responses shifted, however, towards either large or small by the second (stage 2) and third (stage 3) test phases. For the control condition, C0, tested with two additional chickens, no such post-discrimination shifts occurred over the three test stages, as expected according to the FR model.

In summary, the data for each chicken studied under either test condition, C1 or condition C2, demonstrate that predicted contextual effects do occur, and they are quite similar to those observed with human subjects. Indeed, the finding of marked context effects on the psychophysical S-R functions in animal psychophysics is all the more important because it corroborates the general assumption of a comparative analysis of perceptual relativity. Thereby the weighting factor k expressing the slope of the changing gradients ($1/k$) was about ten times higher with the chickens than previously found with human adults (evolutionary relevance).

Further animal data

Figure 3.11 shows the results obtained from an additional investigation with six chickens (*within*-design findings; see Sarris, 1990, 2004). Each of the single trends depicts the values for one subject as a function of both ascending and descending contextual test series. Note, for example, that chickens no. 18 and no. 19 were trained with the same middle-sized training stimuli, but tested with the ascending and descending contextual series (or vice versa). Besides some negligible interindividual differences between the chickens' contextual test-series data, the lawful findings for all of the ascending versus descending PSI trends are of major interest. Indeed, they support once again the overall prediction that such contextual effects are found not only in humans but also in chickens. In other words, these asymmetrical test-series shift (transposition) trends constitute striking examples of systematic frame-of-reference trends for both human and animal psychophysics.

A historical note

It is also of historical interest that Kurt Koffka (1922) had already discussed the general problem of ascending versus descending *shifting* perceptual

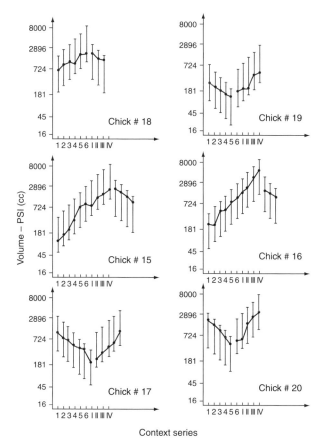

Figure 3.11 Mean PSI trends for six chickens, each trained under identical conditions, but tested systematically with different ascending and descending context stimulus series. The PSI values (ordinata) increase for the
ascending test series and decrease for the descending test series
(abscissa), as predicted by the model. The arabic numbers on the
abscissa indicate the direction of the first context-series shift; the
roman numerals refer to the respective changes in shift direction.
(Adapted from Sarris, 1990, 2004.)

"levels" (frames of reference), at least for human perception (see already
Hollingworth, 1910). Take, for instance, the following quotation from his
classic paper on gestalt psychology published more than 80 years ago in the
Psychological Bulletin:

In reacting to a definite scale of stimuli we establish a general [indifference]
level . . . The effect of each stimulus is dependent upon this level, much
as the figure is dependent upon its ground . . . This level adapts itself

automatically to the [changing] scale of stimuli (which may increase or decrease).

(Koffka, 1922, p. 580; quoted after Sarris, 1990; for a fuller account of Koffka's original idea see Sarris, 1975, 1990)

It also deserves mentioning that such contextual test-series trends can be considered as special transposition effects first studied, albeit on a rudimentary small-scale basis, by Wolfgang Köhler with chimpanzees and chickens (see Köhler, 1951). Thus, the present data point to a convergence of the classical frame-of-reference reasoning (see Spence, 1937; Wertheimer, 1959), on the one hand, and modern comparative psychophysical work, on the other.

Remarks

It should be emphasized that the chicks' contextual test-phase behaviour was lawful, according to a regular psychophysical behaviour. This test behaviour (*between*-subjects design) occurred also on an individual (*within*-subjects design) test-performance level as found in the author's follow-up work. Interestingly, not during the very first test trials (test stage 1), but only with further testing (test stages 2 and 3), did the animals shift their test responses gradually towards the new stimulus series (see Figure 3.8). Note again that this gradual S-R shifting during the test stages occurred as a function of the volume size of the contextual test boxes, in line with the test-data trends found for the human participants. The contextual shifting, however, observed in the chickens occurred at a much slower rate than for the human subjects. This finding is probably due to the fact that the amount of training needed to reach the respective learning criterion of 95 per cent correct responding was much larger for the non-human animals than for human participants. These comparative context effects reflect the perceptual-cognitive nature of the respective psychophysical shifts, and they must not be confused with the so-called *peak shift* phenomenon often found in animal experimentation, which arises from the excitation-inhibition interaction in the animal's reinforcement history (see Thomas, 1993; Urcuioli, 2003).

Multidimensional psychophysics

For the multidimensional case of psychophysical context effects – say, for stimuli varying in both size and colour – three different types have been assumed to be possible (see Figure 3.8):

- *Type I*, which means that subjects perform their choices using only one dimension, i.e., the size values and ignoring the colour dimension completely.
- *Type II*, which implies the subject's one-to-one responding, i.e., the training and test stimulus similarity, in line with its training behaviour.

- *Type III*, which means that the subject takes into separate account the size and the colour dimension (Hauf & Sarris, 2001a, 2001b; Sarris, Hofer, & Zoeke, 1990; see below the example for the chicken's choice behaviour in the two-modality case; the age-related case for humans is presented in chapter 4).

A simple illustration highlights the problem at hand. Everybody knows that jockeys are usually "small" and basketball players "tall"; but at the same time we are able to judge a particular jockey as being relatively large or a basketball player as being relatively short. How do we develop such internal two-dimensional scales and, by means of analogy, how do birds perform in such a task? Considering the fact that most natural objects differ in more than one stimulus dimension the question is raised how animals respond to stimuli differing not in one but two dimensions. Typical frame-of-reference models have neglected this problem almost completely. This neglect is all the more surprising since the analysis of reactions to two or more separable object dimensions (modalities) offers an interesting field for studying the question whether the respective stimulus control of humans differs from that of animals (see example).

EXAMPLE

Animal psychophysics: Two-dimensional size estimation (4A2FC)

Looking for a similar simple task Sarris's research group employed a postdiscrimination-generalization paradigm appropriate for low subhuman animals, with the *size* of cubes as a quantitative dimension and their *colour* as a qualitative variable (Hauf & Sarris, 2001a, 2001b; Sarris, et al., 1990). Thus, this experiment has investigated the influence of a two-dimensional discrimination training, where the chicken had to learn a competitive frame of reference problem, on a unidimensional test (*red* or *green* cubes).

Method

Subjects

Six Leghorn chickens, six weeks old at the beginning of the experiment, served as subjects. The chickens were kept as a flock in a scratching pen. Food was withheld for 8 hours prior to testing; water was continuously available.

Apparatus and stimulus materials

Figure A1.1 (Appendix 1) shows the computer-controlled apparatus permitting the successive presentation of the three-dimensional objects, i.e., different-sized cubes.

The training stimuli were red and green cubes differing in volume. All subjects were trained with two pairs of training stimuli (45/181 ccm red and 724/2896 ccm green cubes). The test stimuli were 7 red, 7 green or 7 grey stimuli equally spaced on a log scale, namely 45, 90.5, 181, 362, 724, 1448, 2896 ccm. The stimuli were presented in front of a $60 \times 60 \times 60$ cm wall on which two pecking keys and two food magazines were fastened, one to the left and the other to the right of the area in which the stimuli were successively shown. The objects were fixed underneath the test box, each on an individual plate, located on a rotary wheel. A motor turned the wheel to the appropriate position, then the plate with the object to be presented was lifted to the floor of the test box.

Procedure

After training to peck the key that was illuminated in order to obtain food, the subjects learned to peck key 1 if 45 ccm red or 724 ccm green was presented, and to peck key 2 if the training stimulus 181 ccm red or 2896 ccm green was shown. Key positions were counterbalanced across subjects. Daily training sessions consisted of 50 trials each. Pecks at the correct key were reinforced by access to the food magazine for 2 s. Darkness immediately followed an incorrect key choice and the same stimulus was presented immediately thereafter (correction-trial). After reaching the learning criterion of 95 per cent correct choices the six subjects were assigned randomly to the two test conditions (green or red cubes). Each series of seven stimuli was presented six times during three test sessions. Each test series was proceeded by a short retraining of 16 trials, and only if the subjects reached a criterion of 14 hits out of 16 trials the test was given. Otherwise retraining was continued. In the test all choices were reinforced.

Results and discussion

Figure 3.12 contains at the left the averaged data of the six chickens investigated and in the middle the single data of the same chickens. As one can easily see the proportions of the large responses differ remarkably depending of the colour of the test series (x–x = red cubes; o–o = green cubes). Note that all six birds investigated perform their judgement according to the "size-colour" rule, i.e. the Type III prediction, repeated at the right of the figure.

These between-session data have been corroborated by new experiments based on within-group testing. In addition, if instead of either red or green

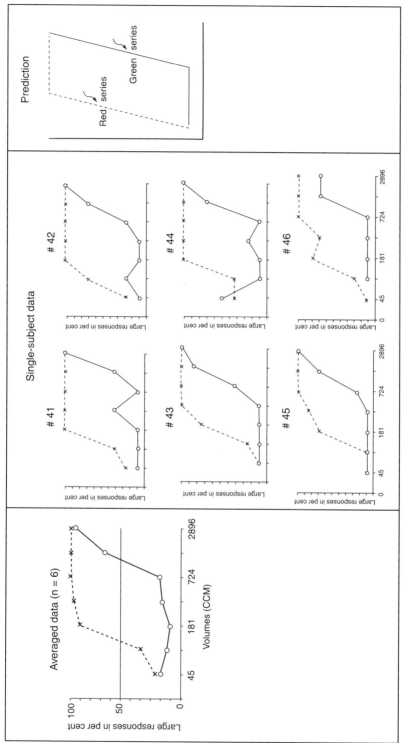

Figure 3.12 Choice data trends for six chickens in the two-modality case (size and colour): psychophysical functions showing generalization effects for one red (x–x) and one green series (o–o) of test cubes differing in size and colour. *Left*: averaged data (n = 6); *middle*: single-subject data; *right* (top): predicted trends (see Type III, Figure 3.8, p. 42). (Adapted from Hauf & Sarris, 2001a, 2001b; Sarris, Hofer & Zoeke, 1990).

objects grey-coloured stimuli are used, the respective psychophysical curve becomes an ogive lying between the red-cube and green-cube trends (Hauf & Sarris, 2001a; Sarris et al., 1990). *This latter finding is all the more remarkable since the chickens had never been trained with the grey colour cubes, but still their grey test data form a most regular S-R trend [sic]!*

Conclusions

Chickens respond to two-dimensional stimuli according to rules which include both the scaling of the quantitative size variable as well as the attention of an additional modality as a cue (i.e., colour). Further studies which aim at the short-term and long-term memory processes underlying such multidimensional categorization-rule behaviour need to be conducted.

Memory and perceptual processes

Most likely, different perceptual memory processes are involved for different animal species during the respective training and test phases. It is also worth mentioning at this point that the memory aspect of this comparative psychophysical work has been further investigated in the author's laboratory by the systematic study of infant chickens' behaviour (baby chicks), thus extending considerably the research presented above (see chapter 4).

Remarks

It must be taken into account that the experimental changes (shifts) in the psychometric functions found for the chickens take place much more slowly than in humans (see Figure 3.13). Again, the main reason for this is probably the enormous amount of training which lower species animals require to learn the discrimination task. This particular memory feature is reflected by the empirical factor k of the FR model that is expressed by Equation 3.1. The putative mechanisms of these memory processes in human and animal psychophysics are discussed elsewhere (see chapter 5; see also Appendix 3, "An Engine Model of Relational Psychophysics").

Furthermore, the studies described above are concerned with one particular type of contextual effect, namely the asymmetry of the variable test series, along with the respective training pair used. Other investigations have demonstrated marked test-stimulus range and frequency contextual effects in humans and in chickens, hence two further types of psychophysical context effects (Figure 3.14). These extended findings for the human and animal subjects in these three different contextual test situations point to the high external validity of the respective comparative psychophysics.

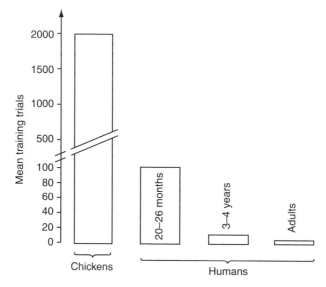

Figure 3.13 Animal and human training data compared. Ordinata: amount of training trials needed. *Left* panel: mean data for chickens (n = 12) trained to discriminate two cube sizes until reaching the learning criterion of 95 per cent correct responses; *right* panel: mean data for humans, that is for human infants (n_1 = 6), 3 to 4-year-old children (n_2 = 6), and adults (n_3 = 10), with the same stimulus-discrimination task. (Adapted from Sarris, 1990, 2004.)

Summary and conclusions

In the past relatively little research was directed toward the joint study of contextual effects in human and animal psychophysics although, considering the present evidence, it is clear that perceptual judgements as studied in comparative psychophysics are basically relational in character. This holds true for humans as well as for non-humans. In other words, the human and animal psychophysics data are quite alike. Nevertheless, it is unclear if – and to which extent – some different mechanisms may be responsible for birds', cats', apes' and humans' transposition performance. The bulk of Sarris and his colleagues' experimental data as presented above illustrates the major ideas and findings which are obtained when behavioural responses, in addition to the subjective judgements (see chapter 2), are collected thus serving to bridge the gaps still existing between the different fields of psychophysics. This complex – and still hotly debated – issue is discussed in chapter 5.

Accordingly, the emphasis in this chapter has concentrated on two aims. The first goal was a consideration of the quantifiable evidence for frame-of-reference effects in the light of a relational approach in psychophysics, on the basis of comparative findings with human and subhuman subjects. The

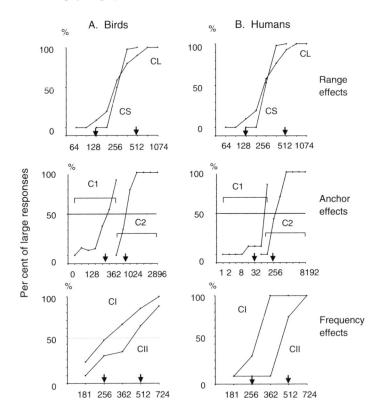

Figure 3.14 Range, asymmetry and frequency context-effect trends for A birds as compared with B humans. The arrows point to the training stimuli. *Top row:* range effects, i.e., response rates for a small (CS) vs. large (CL) test-stimulus range; *middle row:* asymmetry (anchor) effects, i.e., response rates for two contrasted asymmetrical test series (C1 vs. C2), either smaller or larger than the training stimuli; *bottom row:* frequency effects, i.e., for psychometric functions with a positively (CI) vs. negatively (CII) skewed frequency distribution of test stimuli. Note the very similar overall context-effect findings for the human and animal subjects. (Adapted from Sarris, 1990.)

second aim has been related to the fruitful application of a general behavioural paradigm as applied to both human and animal – unidimensional and multidimensional – psychophysics. In respect to the latter aim it became particularly important to appreciate the relevance of memory processes underlying the overt behavioural responses.

4   Developmental psychophysics

If epistemology is to become scientific it will have to learn not only from neurophysiology and physiological psychology but also from developmental (genetic) psychology and from whatever evolutionary biology has to say about cognition.

(Bunge 1983, p. 8)

Introduction

The ideas and findings as described above are extended now to developmental work in comparative psychophysics. The term *developmental psychophysics* refers to the age-specific, cross-sectional and/or longitudinal, case in sensation, perception, and cognition. Here more recent results obtained by the author's research group with young humans and infant birds are outlined and evaluated. In particular, the question is raised here: *To what extent do these developmental findings enrich ongoing and future research in comparative perception and psychophysics?*

An odyssey in developmental psychophysics

In her book on *An Odyssey in Learning and Perception* (1991) the pioneer psychologist Eleanor J. Gibson has reviewed her 50 years of research work in developmental and general experimental psychology with refreshing openness, including the ups and downs of her own achievements. Also today it is of interest to learn about the respective shortcomings and virtues of psychophysical methodology as applied to age-related research problems in human and animal perception. At the same time, Gibson has acknowledged the "explosive" advancements of modern human infant research methodology since the 1980s (see for instance Bornstein, 1999; Gottlieb & Krasnegor, 1985). Indeed, her work may be seen as a milestone in modern developmental research on human and even of animal perception (see Gibson, 1983; Gibson & Pick, 2000). Today the research methodology on perceptual development in infants, both human and animal, might greatly profit from the extension of the research agenda in sensory psychophysics as provided, for example by Davida Y. Teller (1983, 1985, 2000) as well as Jeanette Atkinson and Oliver Braddick (1999; Atkinson, 2000).

Comparative psychophysics and related work

In line with the volumes edited by Mark A. Berkley and William C. Stebbins (1990) *Comparative Perception: Basic Mechanisms*, and more specifically by R.J. Andrew (1991) *Neural and Behavioural Plasticity: The Use of the Domestic Chick as a Model* some major research paradigms of today's, and perhaps also tomorrow's, psychophysics with other animals are of basic interest here. Furthermore, *Perception, Cognition, and Development* (Thomas J. Tighe and Bryan E. Shepp 1983) provides several landmark examples of the substantial interactions among the fields of comparative perception and cognition (e.g., Estes, 1983; Gibson, 1983; Pick, 1983; Spiker & Cantor, 1983). The more recent handbook article by Carolyn Rovee-Collier and Rachel Barr (2001) contains a collection of the methods currently in use for the age-related work on human infant perception and cognition (see also Bremner & Fogel, 2001; De Loache, 2004; Piaget, 1969, 1973; Rovee-Collier, Hayne & Colombo, 2000; Slater, 1998, 2001; Spelke, 1998; Woodward, 2003). It is worth noting, however, that the widely scattered literature of ongoing animal compared to infant work is difficult to evaluate in a theoretically straightforward way.

Developmental psychophysics in Frankfurt

The developmental findings of both human and animal investigations are presented here as a natural extension of this author's earlier work. Ever since the age-specific psychophysical studies in Frankfurt were conducted together with Sarris's former junior colleagues Friedrich Wilkening (1976; Wilkening & Sarris, 1975), Birsen Cangöz (1999), Kirsten Dassler (2000; Dassler & Sarris, 1997), Petra Hauf (2001; Hauf & Sarris, 1999, 2001) and others, one of the key questions of how to explain the biopsychological nature of "contextual" shift effects became an urgent issue. In this context it should be emphasized that our respective age-specific investigations with human participants on lifted weight, volume, area size and time estimations were all carried out in a *game-playing* mode of experimentation (Figure 4.1).

Age-related studies: humans (*Homo sapiens*)

The following developmental findings of cube size and time judgements have demonstrated some basic, i.e., lawful, psychophysical context-effect differences for various human age groups (Figure 4.2). The size-estimation results point to some critical age-specific differences concerning the perceptual-cognitive processes in humans. Very similar developmental context effects

A Bricklaying game   B Washing-day game

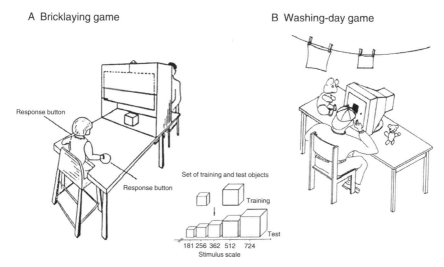

Figure 4.1 Examples of the equipment used in the age-specific studies with human
participants, conducted in a participant-friendly game-like mode. A The
bricklaying game apparatus (*left*) for cube-size estimation with one and the
same training and test stimuli used. B The washing-day game (*right*), for
the analogous study of square-size judgements. (Adapted from Dassler,
2000.)

have been found in other tasks, for instance, in those with time-duration
judgements (Cangöz, 1999; Sarris & Schnehage-Poci, 2004; see Figure 4.3).

The sets of age-related data contained in Figures 4.2 and 4.3 should be
compared with those of Figure 3.5 stemming from the respective adult
group of participants (see also Figure 3.7). Note in particular that the
younger-children groups show much less *transposition* with the more extreme
asymmetry contexts (see Figure 2.3, p. 28: the *Sarris effect*).

Related findings and some caveats

It is tempting to relate the foregoing findings to the work done by other
researchers in the past. For instance, Peter Bryant, Cambridge (UK) already
pointed to the children's *relative codes* of their perceptual behaviour. What
young children remember about perceived objects is always based on its
relationships to the given context (Bryant, 1974; see also Bower, 1966, 1977).
On the other hand, until now there have been only a few psychophysical
studies grounded on age-related parametric experimentation as, for instance,
Friedrich Wilkening (1976, 1982) has initiated (see also Wilkening, Sarris
& Heller, 1972; Wilkening & Anderson, 1982; Wilkening, Levin & Druyan,
1987; Levin & Wilkening, 1989). For the sake of simplicity the theoretical
interpretation of the age-related context shifts as studied in Sarris's research
group is postponed (see chapter 5). Note here that most models of comparative

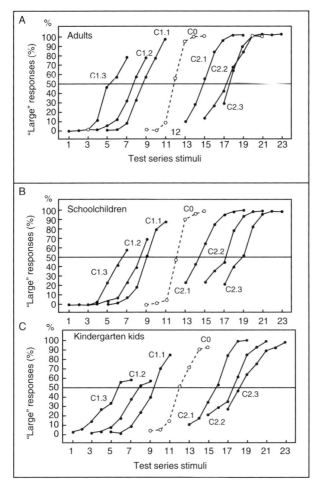

Figure 4.2 Psychophysical size-estimation data for A human adults, B elementary school children, and C preschoolers (kindergarten children). Note that the age-specific mean data trends are very similar. However, the age-specific inter- and intra-individual variability is highly different. (Adapted from Dassler, 2000.)

choice behaviour are moot on the biopsychological processes by which the age-related *relational* choice regularities may arise.

Age-specific context shifts: two basic facts

At this point it may be safely stated that in general Sarris's ontogenetic findings with hundreds of human participants, all trained and tested in individual experimental sessions, carry two basic characteristic features, namely:

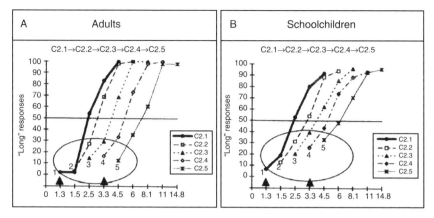

Figure 4.3 Psychophysical time-estimation data for: A human adults compared with those from B schoolchildren. There are important age-specific context-effect limits. (Adapted from Cangöz, 1999.)

1   *Amount of context shifts.* Typically, the psychophysical context-effect shifts are very much larger for younger than for older human participants, notwithstanding the fact that the more global (overall) statistical mean PSI shifts of the younger age groups, i.e., 2 to 4 years and older children, may qualitatively look much alike. These cross-sectional findings should be compared with some – still lacking – *longitudinal* data sets (see also Brainerd, 1981, 1983; Brainerd & Reyna, 1990, 1993, 1994).

2   *Amount of shift variability.* The inter- and intra-individual context-shift variability ("instability") is much higher for the young and very young age groups than for the older and adult participants, respectively

The following example illustrates some crucial *multidimensional* context effects in age-related human psychophysics (Hauf, 2001).

EXAMPLE

Human psychophysics: Two-dimensional size estimation (4A2FC)

In Frankfurt's psychophysics laboratory, Petra Hauf has conducted several systematic multidimensional context-shift (transposition) experiments with different age groups. Her major findings illustrate important performance-strategy changes in developmental psychophysics. For instance, in her extensive studies with children Hauf (2001) has provided reliable evidence for three different age-related perceptual judgement strategies, in contrast to the results obtained from our analogue studies with birds (see Figure 3.13).

In her two-dimensional psychophysical research – size and colour judgements with four different age groups – the longstanding developmental hypothesis was tested if, and to what extent, three different judgement strategies were employed during the test stage of post-discrimination generalization (see Figure 3.8). Theoretically, these age-specific perceptual judgements could be based either on only one dominant dimension, e.g., size (*Type I*), or on the perceptual *similarity* between the two-dimensional training and the one-dimensional test stimuli (*Type II*), or on both dimensions (*Type III*). In Hauf's experiments the context-induced judgements of different figure sizes were analysed depending on variable colour in one condition and on variable brightness in the other. As stated above, the main objective was the study of the age-related development of the different hypothesized two-dimensional judgement strategies.

Method

A total of 144 participants of four age groups (4-year-olds, 8-year-olds, 12-year-olds, and 18-year-olds) were trained and tested individually. During training the discrimination of a set of two-dimensional psychophysical stimuli was learned by means of a two-choice task (training phase); two-dimensional stimulus-generalization tests were presented afterwards (test phase). About half of the participants were trained and tested under a colour-size context condition, the rest under a brightness-size context condition.

Apparatus and materials

A slide projector with a screen was used, along with a board containing two response keys. By pressing the corresponding button (e.g., "small" = left button, "large" = right button), the participant had to judge the successively presented stimulus sizes (*fairy tale* figures; see Figure 4.4). Hence, the training and test stimuli were either blue or green in colour. During training the participant learned first the discrimination between the "small blue" versus the "large blue" stimulus, on the one hand, and subsequently the "small green" versus the "large green" object, on the other hand (or vice versa). During the test phase all the sizes in both colours were presented, one after the other (*4A2FC* paradigm; randomized permutation).

Note that the smaller ones of each stimulus pair belonged together in one and the same small category and the larger ones in the large category relative to the entire stimulus set. During the tests, all sizes in both colours were presented, one after the other (the marked numbers 1 and 3 and 7 and 9 in Figure 4.4 refer to the four training stimuli).

Results and discussion

The major results of these two-dimensional experiments with the four age groups investigated are summarized in Figure 4.5. Basically, for these age

Set of training and test-stimuli

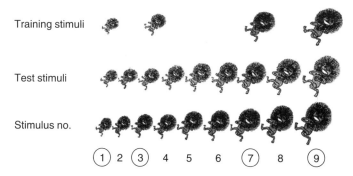

Training stimuli

Test stimuli

Stimulus no.

(1) 2 (3) 4 5 6 (7) 8 (9)

Figure 4.4 Two-dimensional training and test stimuli (fairy tale figures) varying in size
with either blue or green colour in the experiments of Hauf (2001) with
human participants of different age. (Adapted from Hauf, 2001.)

groups all three predicted types of judgemental strategies were obtained,
i.e., no fundamental qualitative age differences were recorded. However,
the adult group had chosen mostly the Type I strategy, second the Type
II alternative (in contrast, the chickens followed exclusively the Type III
strategy; see Figure 3.8, p. 42). The above findings illustrate the main fact that
the multidimensional (here: two-dimensional) extension of the *2A2FC*
paradigm provides ample data for a multiple perceptual-cognitive strategy
during the post-discrimination generalization phase within all the age groups
studied here.

At first sight it appears that the Type III strategy is the most complex
("difficult") one. Therefore it is all the more astonishing that chickens adhere
to this response type (see Figure 3.12): What is the comparative explanation
for these findings? One straightforward answer to this question is that during
the long training phase the chickens have learned to keep the size and colour
dimensions *separate* and during testing they stick to this well-memorized
distinction. In stark contrast, the adult humans mostly show a flexible choice
strategy. It should be also noted that the 4-yr-old children preferred different
judgement strategies for the colour (Type I) versus brightness (Type II) condition for as yet unknown reasons (see also Hauf, 2001; Hauf & Sarris, 2001a,
2001b; Parducci, Knobel, & Thomas, 1976; see furthermore Coren & Enns,
1993; Coren & Miller, 1974; DiLollo, Enns, & Rensink, 2002; Mandler, 2000,
2004; Zur Oeveste, 1987).

Further systematic research needed

There remain at least three major requirements for future research in this
kind of human multidimensional psychophysics:

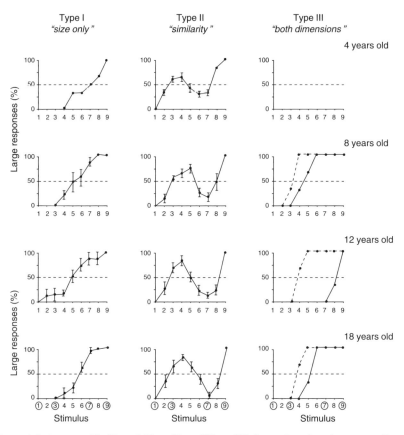

Figure 4.5 Age-specific Type I, Type II and Type III size-estimation data according to the two-dimensional experiments of Hauf (2001) with four different age groups (4 years old, 8 years old, 12 years old, 18 years old). (Adapted from Hauf, 2001.)

1   Until hitherto Petra Hauf's 4A2FC paradigm has been investigated only for symmetrical but not for asymmetrical test-series stimuli. In other words, there is a strong need to extend the present multidimensional research to the case of *asymmetrical* context conditions, analogously to the unidimensional transposition studies as described in chapter 3.

2   There is a need for extensive work also with preverbal children, say for the first two or three years of human development (for some standard methods used to train and test human infants see Table 4.1; see also Gierlatzek, 1985; Heiss, 1984). Indeed, it is tempting to speculate about the cognitive strategies employed by human infants. In fact, the present research paradigm could, nay should, be adapted to the infant case, employing the conjugate reinforcement paradigm developed and extensively applied by Carolyn Rovee-Collier in her studies with game

Table 4.1 Some of the standard methods used to test human infants. Note that the method being closest to Sarris's research with children is the operant conditioning technique. (Adapted from Rookes & Willson, 2000.)

Method	Description	Assumption
Conditioning a head-turning response (*operant conditioning*)	The baby is rewarded (e.g., by being shown a colourful toy every time she/he looks at a particular stimulus.	If the stimulus is shown among other stimuli and the baby continues to indicate a preference for it, it is assumed that she/he can distinguish it.
Eye-movement monitoring	The baby's eye movements are recorded photographically during the scanning of visual stimuli.	If the baby only focuses on a single or limited number of features (e.g., the contours), it is assumed that she/he cannot perceive the whole figure.
Preferential looking	This method, sometimes called "spontaneous visual preference" technique, involves the simultaneous presentation of two visual stimuli.	If the infant looks at one stimulus for longer than at the other, it is inferred that: • the baby can distinguish between the two • the baby prefers one stimulus over the other.
Habituation ("familiarity")	This method is used when the baby distinguishes between two stimuli (there is no visual preference for one of them); it is used when she/he loses interest and stops looking.	If the infant starts looking at the novel stimulus having habituated to the old one, the researcher concludes that she/he can tell the difference between the two.
Sucking rate	The baby is given a dummy and the sucking rate is measured in response to different visual stimuli: after prolonged stimulus exposure, habituation will occur.	If there is a change in sucking rate when a novel stimulus is presented, it is assumed that the baby can distinguish between the two stimuli.
Heart and breathing rate	The baby's heart and/or breathing rate is monitored for changes when novel stimuli are presented.	If there is a change in rate, the researcher concludes that the baby can recognize the new stimulus as being different.
Visually evoked potentials (VEPs)	Electrodes are attached to the baby's scalp to measure electrical brain activity; certain stimulus-correlated patterns occur in response to visual stimuli.	If different VEPs are recorded in response to different visual stimuli, it is assumed that the infant is distinguishing between them.

mobiles (e.g., Rovee-Collier & Barr, 2001; Rachel Barr, personal communication, November 2003). For example, by implementing colour and size variations in mobiles between training and test phases, it might be possible to examine the infants' generalization-transposition strategies.

3   It is also important to analyse the *working memory* processes involved in the 2A2FC and 4A2FC paradigms of developmental perception and psychophysics. Among other things the question is: How does the frontal lobe of the infant's developing brain assist in age-related perceptual-cognitive information processing? Moreover, the monkey infant – say, the chimpanzee and galago monkey with an assumed more primitive frontal lobe – should be confronted with the same uni-dimensional and two-dimensional tasks as successfully investigated in the present work (Goldman-Rakic, 1988; Patricia Goldman-Rakic, personal communication, January 1997; Mortimer Mishkin, personal communication, March 1996; see also chapter 6). Another methodological point is related to the *instruction*-specific changes of the different strategies used. The older children and especially the adult participants seem to be very flexible in applying all three judgement types of strategies; for instance, the Type III strategy was more or less frequently used during the test phases depending on the given instructional set (see Valkenburg, Hauf, & Sarris, 2000; Vonhausen, Hauf, Sczepansky, & Sarris, 1998).

Until today the developmental, i.e., age-related perceptual differences between different human age groups are not well understood in the sense of a rigorous *explanatory* neurobiological interpretation. Presumably the systematic study of much younger children – say, aged between 15 months to 3 years old – will provide even more relevant data to help explain Petra Hauf's findings systematically (see Maddox, 2002, on *separable* and *integral* intermodal/multidimensional information integration; see also Bahrick, 1992, 2000; Baillargeon, 1993; Hauf & Baillargeon, 2005; Karmiloff-Smith, 1992; Markman & Ross, 2003). As stated above, at least for human infants, the enormous intra- and inter-individual *dynamic* variability (instability) of the perceptual-cognitive performance may be of greater biopsychological relevance than the age-specific mean differences (see also below the infant chickens' data).

Age-related studies: baby chicks (*Gallus gallus domesticus*)

As cited at the beginning of this book (chapter 1, p. 8), Lucia Regolin and her research team in Padova, Italy, have studied the infant chick's perceptual-cognitive behaviour extensively from a gestalt psychological perspective. Thereby, the infant chick is considered a most important model of developmental research (Regolin, Tommasi, & Vallortigara, 2000; Regolin & Vallortigara, 1995, 2003; see also Andrew, 1991; Rogers, 1995).

Nowadays the ontogeny of perceptual relativity is becoming a central issue in comparative research on animal and human cognitive development. The common assumption of most frame-of-reference models is and remains that subjects choose between discriminative stimuli during the training and testing phases not so much on the basis of their absolute, but rather on the basis of their relative physical properties. This fact is nicely illustrated by the contextually induced shifts of choice behaviour during the post-discrimination generalization phase in the baby chick too: Previous studies have shown that during *standard* training the colour discrimination was learned much faster than during the size-discrimination task (e.g., Sarris, 1990, 1994, 1998). However, more recently the research question has been extended as follows: *Do there exist both relative and absolute response tendencies in the young chick's choice behaviour?*

The following example contains the findings of several transposition studies with infant chickens as conducted in the author's animal laboratory; for more details the reader may consult the original reports (Hauf, Sarris, & Prior, 2005; Sarris, 1998; Sarris, Hauf, & Arlt, 2001).

EXAMPLE

Infant animal psychophysics: Unidimensional colour and size estimations

In our earlier research with the standard training method it had been observed that whereas there were more absolute choice responses with colour, the chick displayed more relative responses with regard to size. The present experiments were conducted to investigate more fully the chicken's ontogeny of colour and size perception in respect to the variable proportions of absolute versus relative choice responses. The main hypothesis was that there is a clear difference in choice behaviour when the infant chick is trained under an *absolute* or *relative* stimulus-presentation condition. Furthermore, whereas the colour dimension should lead to more absolute choice responses, more relative choices should be observed when the size dimension is used.

Method

Animals

Altogether, $N_1 = 24$ and $N_2 = 22$ White Leghorn chicks (*Gallus gallus domesticus*), one day old at the start of the experiments, were kept as a flock in a scratching pen with a natural light/dark cycle. The infant chicks were mildly deprived of food. However, water was available ad lib. For one of the two groups ($N_1 = 24$), 16 chicks participated in the reinforcer-efficiency and colour-generalization experiment with the standard training procedure. In addition, eight chicks served as subjects in the context-effect study of size discrimination. For the other group ($N_2 = 22$), the chickens were trained to discriminate either between two different coloured (green vs. blue) or two different sized (small vs. large) stimuli. The training was absolute or relative and it consisted always of four stimulus pairs (nos. 3 & 5, 5 & 7, 1 & 5, 5 & 9; see Table 4.2).

General procedure: Multiple reinforcer conditions

The apparatus is shown in Figure 4.6. The simultaneous-discrimination training (standard condition) started on the first day of life. The baby chick was waiting in the dark (resting) part of the rectangular test apparatus, i.e., either in chamber 1 or chamber 2. Then the partition wall was lifted, thus giving access to the second illuminated compartment containing the two training stimuli (TS).

In order to enhance rapid approaches to the TS, short sequences of "maternal" calls were emitted by two loudspeakers mounted under the respective two stimulus objects, which were light-coloured cardboard cubes standing on feeders. The cubes were pushed away when pecked by a chick thus allowing for 5 seconds free access to the *food* and, at the same time, to the delivery of *warmth* and *maternal call* as positive reinforcers. The use of either colour or size of the TS objects in different subgroups was counterbalanced

Table 4.2 Experimental sets of training and test stimuli for the infant chicken's "relative" versus "absolute" task conditions (*simultaneous* stimulus presentation). The materials were constructed from nine stimulus values (1, 2, 3 . . . 8, 9) of the size or colour dimension. Shown are the rank-order values of the pairs of training stimuli and those of the subsequent test series. The "relative" training condition consisted of four stimulus pairs (3 & 5, 5 & 7, 1 & 5, 5 & 9); thereby, the stimulus with the larger number was always reinforced. In contrast, during the "absolute" training condition one and the same stimulus pairs were used; however, the stimulus *No. 5* was always reinforced. Throughout the test sessions each stimulus was presented paired with each other (*bold letters*: reinforced training stimuli).

Stimuli	1	2	3	4	5	6	7	8	9
"Relative" training			3		**5**				
					5		**7**		
	1				5				
					5				**9**
Test series C0	1		3		5		7		9
"Absolute" training			3		**5**				
					5		7		
			3		**5**				
					5				9
Test series C0	1		3		5		7		9

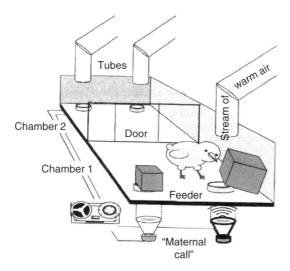

Figure 4.6 Two-choice apparatus used to train and test infant chickens with size and/or colour stimuli, with the two chambers 1 (*front*) and 2 (*back*). Multiple-reinforcement equipment: (a) two air-path tubes ("stream of warm air"); (b) two loudspeakers ("maternal" call); (c) two feeders. (Adapted from Sarris, 1998.)

across the infant chicks (for the stimulus materials see Figure 4.7; example: standard training). Whereas a correct choice always led to the positive multiple reinforcement, an incorrect choice was immediately followed by darkness (non-reinforcement). Throughout the training session the subsequent trial was switched from one chamber (e.g., *front*) to the other one (e.g., *background*) of the experimental apparatus. Each training session lasted about 15 minutes. On the first day of life three daily sessions were provided; beginning with day two, four sessions per day were employed.

Generalization and context-effect testing

After reaching the criterion of 70 per cent correct responses in two successive training sessions, generalization testing started. Figure 4.7 shows the test stimuli for the three series C0, C1 and C2 used in separate sessions. Each object of the test-stimulus set was presented three times whereas each trial consisted of one of the contextual test stimuli including the unrewarded TS. Note that during the C0, C1 or C2 testing phase every choice was reinforced. The test-series sessions started always with 10 retraining trials followed by 12 test trials; thereafter, 5 retraining trials were provided.

Each test series consisted of five cubes in ascending volume by equal geometric steps; i.e., condition C0, the no-context control condition, was symmetrically constructed whereas the contextual conditions C1 and C2 were asymmetrically arranged around the respective TS (see Figure 4.7). During

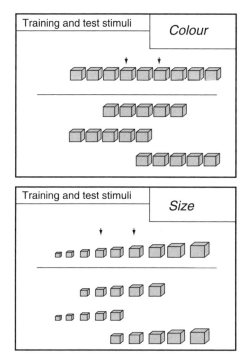

Figure 4.7 Schematic overview of the training and test stimuli for the infant chick studies, in geometric steps of volume size, CCM (see text). (Adapted from Sarris, 1998.)

the absolute training condition the stimulus no. 5 was always reinforced. However, during relative training the stimulus with the larger rank-order number was always reinforced (see Table 4.2, p. 66). Throughout the training each correct choice led to a multiple reinforcement consisting of warmth, maternal call and food access. Again, as stated above, a wrong choice was followed by a short period of darkness which lasted until the next trial started. Analogously to the standard training as previously used (e.g., Sarris, 1998) all infant chicks were trained individually according to a 70 per cent criterion in two successive sessions. Only the chicks which had reached the training criterion during two successive sessions were tested. Note that only 12 out of 22 chicks passed this test criterion (N_{train} = 22, but N_{test} = 12).

Results and discussion

Training data

Figure 4.8 shows the differences between the training-performance curves obtained for the absolute and relative training conditions. The per cent-correct

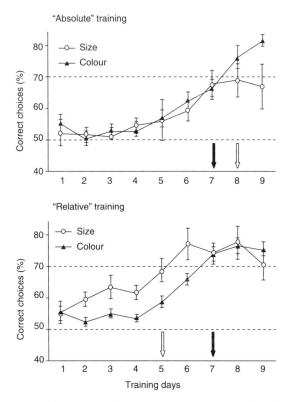

Figure 4.8 Training performance curves for the "absolute" and "relative" simultaneous training conditions. (Adapted from Hauf, Sarris, & Prior, 2005.)

responses (ordinate) reveal the fact that the chickens of the colour-discrimination task reached the test criterion during the absolute training much faster than baby chicks participating in the size-discrimination task; i.e., they show a significantly higher performance level. In addition, this modality-specific difference was also found for those chickens that had obtained the relative training task. In this case the chickens of the size-discrimination task learned more efficiently. In other words, the training performance shows a special interaction for colour and size. Namely, the 70 per cent criterion was reached significantly more often under the "colour-absolute" condition as compared with the other training conditions. Apparently, under the absolute condition colour discrimination seems to be easier for the baby chick than size discrimination.

Test data (main findings)

According to the general prediction, the test data illustrate some substantial context effects, first for the standard training condition (see Figure 4.9 for one

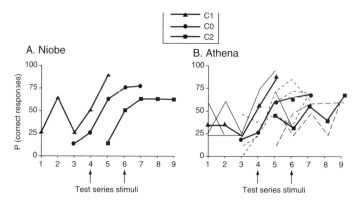

Figure 4.9 Post-discrimination individual test data for two infant chicks, obtained under standard training investigated under the context conditions C0, C1, and C2: A data for *Niobe*, with very regular contextual shift curves; B *Athena*, with noisy data trends. (Adapted from Sarris, Hauf, & Arlt, 2001.)

individual infant chick, Niobe, with very regular context shift curves as contrasted with the experimentally noisy trends for another chick, Athena). More importantly, the test data also show highly significant differences as to the proportions of absolute versus relative choice behaviour. The absolute training was more often followed by absolute choice behaviour during generalization testing, whereas relative choices occurred most frequently after relative training (Figure 4.10). Interestingly, these differences are more pronounced in the case of the colour dimension, i.e., the chickens with the colour-discrimination task responded mostly in absolute terms, but those with the size-discrimination task showed a higher portion of relative responses (see also Figure 4.11 with so-called *preference scores*, i.e., predominant choices varying between −1 and +1). In other words, not only the training data but also the test-performance findings illustrate some important modality-specific effects (which are probably of ecological-evolutionary relevance).

Conclusions

The absolute and relative colour and size data are based on the experimental comparison of an absolute versus relative stimulus-presentation procedure as contrasted to the traditional standard presentation technique used during the discrimination-training phase. In contrast to the previous standard-training findings (see Sarris et al., 2001, Figure 3), the present training curves are differentially affected in that the infant chicks learned at least the colour task much faster under the absolute condition, but the size task better under the relative condition. The training and test results make important biopsychological (*evolutionary*) sense with regard to the modality-specific information processing involved. This interaction between the two sensory

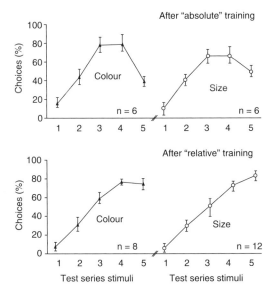

Figure 4.10 Test choices in per cent for the different training conditions: the infant chicks show more absolute choices after "absolute" training (*top*) and more absolute choices for the colour (*left*) than for the size (*right*) dimension. The data curves reflect the transition from mainly absolute choices with colour after absolute training (*top left*) to a curve indicating more relative choices with size after relative training (*bottom right*). (Adapted from Hauf, Sarris, & Prior, 2005.)

modalities – *size* and *colour* – and the different training procedures is well reflected by the test-data trends (*awakening cognition*).

The additional findings for the *successive,* instead of the *simultaneous,* training and testing procedure are of special interest because successive discrimination learning is a much harder task (see Figure 4.12). How are the 2 × 2, i.e., the four context-shift data trends for the colour versus size and the simultaneous versus successive conditions best explained? There are at least two main ecological-evolutionary interpretations of these findings of interest here:

1   *Size versus colour coding.* Whereas size as such is a perceptual-cognitive modality and therefore more context dependent, colour is much more a sensory-coded modality and hence less context dependent (Figure 4.12, top right vs. top left).

2   *Successive versus simultaneous stimulus coding.* In contrast to the successive discrimination task, the simultaneous stimulus presentation involves much more sensory coding and is therefore much less context dependent (tentatively, see the *binding problem:* e.g., Engel & Singer, 2001; Engel, Fries, & Singer, 2001; Singer, 1999, 2004; more specifically and critically

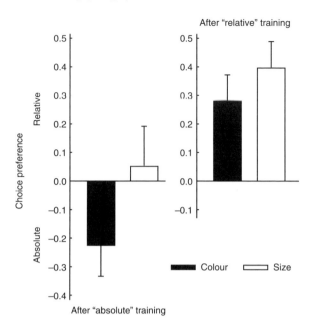

Figure 4.11 Preference-score data for the infant chickens reflecting the distinction between an absolute and relative choice strategy: strict preference of the absolute strategy leads to a score of −1 as opposed to the relative strategy with a maximum score of +1. (Adapted from Hauf, Sarris, & Prior, 2005.)

see Farid, 2002; Hommel, 2004). In other words, the successive coding which requires more stimulus-memory capacity is more context dependent, which is in accordance with, for instance, Elfering's (1997; see here Figure 3.6) context-shift findings in human perception (Figure 4.12: bottom left vs. bottom right).

Thus, the findings illustrated in Figure 4.12 are a rare but extremely important example of *ecological-evolutionary* information coding in the chicken.

Comparative methodological issues

Our comparative findings of context shifts in developmental psychophysics are based on the general rationale as outlined above (see chapter 3). The following methodological issues illustrate the conceptual and empirical problems involved in this research with infant animals:

Current methodological demands

One of these methodological issues refers to the relatively huge intra- and inter-individual variability in the infant chick's training and test performance

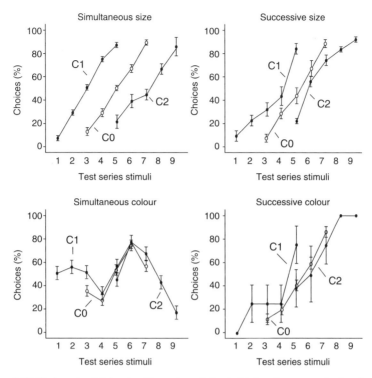

Figure 4.12 Data sets obtained with various infant chick subgroups: A simultaneous stimulus presentation; B successive stimulus presentation. (Sarris, Hauf, Prior, & Schnehage-Poci, 2003; unpubl. data.)

as contrasted to that of older chickens. In fact, only the unique methodical care made the discovery of the baby chick's transposition capacity possible as shown above. As to the statistical data analysis it was necessary to distinguish between so-called *signal* versus *signal-plus-noise* performance (Figure 4.13). Note that these (signal) results are free from unwarranted intra- and inter-individual noise (i.e., the random behavioural responses within and between the subjects had been removed; see Hauf, et al., 2005). Such findings should be evaluated also in light of longitudinal research work (e.g., Teller, 2000, Figure 6.3; Thelen & Smith, 1994).

Furthermore, it should be kept in mind that all of these comparative and developmental findings have been obtained by the use of a specific experimental paradigm, i.e., special training and testing techniques (for the human infant case, see also De Loache, 2004; Gierlatzek, 1985; Heiss, 1984). In this context the reader is referred to the different alternative methods being currently in use in human infant research (see Table 4.1, p. 63). Naturally, the same point holds in the infant animal case. For instance, Teller's (2000) approach to establishing the validity of infant monkeys as an animal model

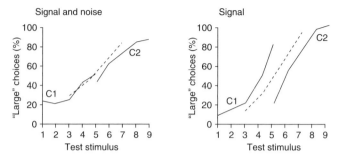

Figure 4.13 "Signal" versus "signal-plus-noise" context-test performance for the size subgroups of infant chickens (the data for the colour subgroups are similar but much "noisier". (Sarris, Hauf, Prior, & Schnehage-Poci, 2004; unpublished data.)

for human sensory development in vision has been to collect developmental data with similar stimuli and techniques from both species. In general, if the two or more species have similar visual capacities and follow similar sequences of developmental change, albeit on different time scales, it should be possible to establish an age-relevant conversion factor between the species (according to Davida Teller, such an age conversion may permit generalization of such results from the monkey infant to the human infant, i.e., to use such data taken on the monkey to model human visual development).

Remarks

It must be kept in mind that the contextual shifts as reported here reflect mostly the so-called asymmetry effects, both with humans and birds. However, if another context parameter is studied, say, the *frequency* factor (e.g., Zoeke, 1987), most likely one will find the opposite developmental trend, at least with human participants (Figure 4.14). Unfortunately, no such psychophysical frequency effects have ever been studied with human infants and comparatively with additional species (e.g., monkeys, cats, fish). Nevertheless, Robert B. Lickliter and Lorraine Bahrick, both at the International University of Florida, Miami, have accomplished fundamental comparative research on prenatal birds' and humans' intermodal development. Their work contributed to a better understanding of the intersensory ("cross-modality") information integration of different modality inputs (e.g., Bahrick, 2000; Lefkowicz & Lickliter, 1994; Lickliter & Bahrick, 2000; Lickliter et al., 2002; see also Spelke, 1998). This latter work, although being beyond the scope of Sarris's research, should be followed up on the basis of parametric *psychophysical* experimentation (for instance, see the study of the *size-weight illusion* in the human infant: conducted by Hauf & Baillargeon, 2005).

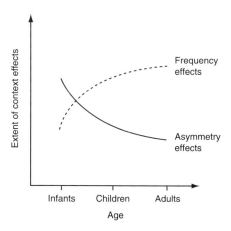

Figure 4.14 Contrasting hypothesized developmental trends for human infants, children, and adults under "asymmetry" (bold) versus "frequency" (dashed curve) context conditions in stimulus-generalization testing. Arguably, one might find such opposite developmental trends, at least with humans. (Adapted from Zoeke, 1987.)

Summary and conclusions

The comparative ideas and findings, as illustrated in chapter 3, have been extended here to some fundamental age-related work in both human and animal psychophysics. Our major results reflect the discovery of age-related multiple judgement strategies as well as developmental contextual shifts in the humans' and chickens' psychophysics. Clearly, these accomplishments do not lead to the establishment of an either–or distinction between absolute versus relative information integration in multidimensional judgements, but rather point to a more or less conception of the human and bird's cognitive psychophysics (which must not be confused with the concept of a comparative sensory/peripheral psychophysics: see Teller, 2000). However, these comparative and developmental findings have not led so far to any safe neurobiological interpretations. Rather they involve the necessity of extended developmental work in the future as to the comparative psychophysics of, for instance, size, colour and time estimation in both the human and the subhuman species. Stated in more positive terms, despite the complex issues involved, the roots of the awakening cognition in the infant chicken have been successfully traced here. At any rate, it is held that the developmental findings greatly enrich the empirical basis for the future of comparative psychophysics.

The following chapter provides a more theory-oriented treatment of relational psychophysics. Thereby, a *multiple-stage* idea concerning the different sensory-perceptual-cognitive processes involved is outlined (*psychophysics beyond sensation*).

5 New perspectives in perceptual-cognitive psychophysics

No treatment of contemporary human and animal psychophysics is complete without at least some mentioning of cognition. The dramatic increase in interest in cognitive processes [may be viewed] as a return to the roots of comparative psychology.

(Dewsbury, 1989, p. 215)

Introduction

Up until now it was widely held, at least among the psychophysicists in human adult perception, that two different, though not incompatible, approaches are equally valid and important. There is, on the one hand, the aim of the sensory psychophysicist: his main target has been and remains the construction of so-called "unbiased" scales and models of sensory-perceptual magnitude, thereby studying specific sensory events such as sensory adaptation and contrast processing. On the other hand, the major goal of many other researchers – including the author's approach – more closely reflects the aim of the cognitive scientist who wants to understand the intertwined processes of perception and judgement, such as perceptual-cognitive context effects and task-dependent influences.

Multi-stage approach in psychophysics

Some contemporary scientists suggest the combination of these two research approaches for more fruitful theorizing and experimentation. For instance, in their handbook article, Lawrence E. Marks, USA and Daniel Algom, Israel emphasize the point that there exist different stage theories or models of psychophysical processing. "[They] . . . acknowledge the possibility . . . that the given *context* can affect processes occurring at every *stage*: in early sensory transduction, in perceptual encoding, possible cognitive recoding, and in decision response" (Marks & Algom 1998, p. 148; emphasis VS). Whereas these and other experts do not suggest any specific model in order to pinpoint the putative information-integration mechanisms involved, a general multi-stage model, as depicted below, is suggested here (see Sarris, 2001a, 2004). Such an approach continues the efforts to understand and model the different "context" processes of psychophysics more fully. Indeed, it addresses the main question: *How should, and really can, present-day and future research go beyond the orientation of the earlier major approaches to psychophysics?*

In the following section this general three-stage process model (Figure 5.1) is outlined on the basis of a weighted *bottom-up* and *top-down* linkage, followed by two subsections on cognitive neuroscience and nonlinear mathematical model building. Note that this chapter provides a theory-oriented treatment of perceptual-cognitive psychophysics, including however some major conceptual caveats.

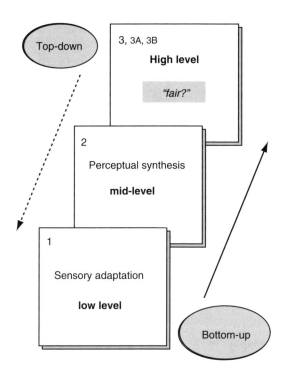

Figure 5.1 A general multiple-stage model of the intertwined mechanisms in perception and psychophysics for the (1) low-level, i.e., sensory information gathering, (2) mid-level, i.e., perceptual information synthesis, and (3) high-level, i.e., (3A) memory-plus-decision and (3B) language functioning. This comparative psychophysics model corresponds to the distinction and linkage of the observed sensory, perceptual, and cognitive "context" effects in behavioural research as correlated with the underlying brain processes. Note that the weight for the bottom-up (bold arrow) processing is stressed much more than that for the top-down (dotted, thin arrow) stream, in the light of a comparative and evolutionary point of view. (Note also the "fair?" question mark, i.e., a caveat sign at the top of the model.)

Multiple-stage processing in perception and psychophysics

The basic assumption here is in line with the main research literature consulted that there are at least three basic interrelated sensory-perceptual-cognitive *process stages*:

- sensory information gathering
- perceptual information synthesis
- memory-plus-decision-making (3A, 3B).

These three putative process stages are intertwined by bottom-up and top-down interactions; and they correspond to the three well-known neuro-biological process levels, namely the *low-level, mid-level* and *high-level* stages of the brain functioning of comparative perception (Figure 5.1). Whereas the hypothetical interplay of bottom-up and top-down processes is nowadays broadly accepted in the cognitive neuroscience community (e.g., Ahissar & Hochstein, 2004; Hochstein & Ahissar, 2002; Kastner, 2004), especially the neurobiological nature of the high-level processing is still hotly debated. Linked to, i.e., causally correlated with, these putative process stages in perception and psychophysics are the main types of the basic contextual phenomena in psychophysics. These effects may be classified tentatively according to the following major classes:

- *Stage 1:* sensory adaptation and contrast effects (low level)
- *Stage 2:* perceptual frame-of-reference and constancy phenomena (mid-level)
- *Stage 3:* cognitive functioning related to memory and decision-making effects (*high level*). (Note as a special subcase in human perception and psychophysics the involvement of *language* and *semantics* in response-scale adjustment.)

Remarks

It is postulated here that many if not all of the various context phenomena in psychophysics represent a complex interplay of different *feed-forward* and *feed-backward* processing effects. For example, there are putative context effects that are based on the processes related mainly to stages 1 plus 2, or stages 2 plus 3 (or even more complex processes, i.e., stages 1, 2 plus 3). For this reason more than just three (stage-) types of context effects are to be assumed. In past research the conceptual emphasis was only on the main process stages 1, 2 or 3 as more or less being related to the ordinary scaling methodology and the so-called psychophysical laws (e.g., Baird, 1970; Parducci, 1982). Interestingly, a lot of the work published during the last 20 years has been concentrated on the contextual problems involved in perceptual-cognitive psychophysics (say, stages 2 plus 3). Also, the *transposition* phenomenon for human and animal psychophysics may be assigned mainly to stages 2 and 3. Note, that the bottom-up conception of this three-stage model is weighted more heavily than the complementary top-down idea due to its basic phylogenetic-ontogenetic nature (see Figure 5.1).

In passing, consider also the so-called *task-set switching phenomenon* and the *hysteresis* effect related to process-relevant cognitive control devices for stage 1, stage 2 and stage 3 (e.g., Goldstone, 2003; Kimchi, 1992, 1998; Parker & Schneider, 1994; Peterson, 1999, 2003; Petrov & Anderson, 2005; Zemel, Behrmann, Mozer, & Bavelier, 2002). Yet the question remains: How can such phenomena be considered to be cognitive "control devices" – are they the unique effects of action of such devices?

Bridges between the putative process stages?

The rationale of this general multiple-stage context model implies some fundamental pro and con ideas, especially the following. On the one hand, this model improves the conceptual status of the widespread "potpourri" attitude in past and present research (e.g., Baird, 1997; Marks & Algom, 1998) in accepting the state-of-the-art understanding of the current diversive knowledge. On the other hand, this approach, resting on a putative basis of reasoning, calls for continuing research efforts for filling in the *gaps* of knowledge concerning the phenomenological, behavioural and neurobiological aspects of perception (see Figure 1.1, p. 7; see also Spillmann & Dresp, 1995; Teller, 1984; Uttal, 1995, 1998). In other words, the ongoing research in comparative perception and psychophysics must develop the status of present theorizing and experimentation, including the perceptual constancy and memory processes involved (see chapter 6).

Another multiple-stage model

George Sperling, University of California, USA, has advanced quite a similar multiple-stage rationale, specifically suggested for visual motion perception (Lu & Sperling, 1996, 2001, 2002; see also Casco, Grieco, & Giora, 2003; Kubovy & Gepshtein, 2003; Marr, 1982, Figure 6–1; Palmer, 2003). Moreover, a similar weighted top-down (high-level) versus bottom-up (low-level) process model or theory for conscious human vision has been recently suggested by Saul Hochstein and Merav Ahissar (Ahissar & Hochstein, 2004; Hochstein & Ahissar, 2002).

Table 5.1 briefly summarizes the major consequences of a top-down (late process) versus bottom-up theory (early process) for conscious human vision. This general tabular scheme is interesting in itself, but admittedly it is silent in respect of the comparative subhuman (*unconscious?*) case of animal perception and psychophysics.

Table 5.1 A "top-down" (high-level, late process) versus "bottom-up" (low-level, early process) theory for conscious human vision as suggested by Hochstein and Ahissar (e.g., 2002). This evidence-based theory is summarized by a tabular scheme; i.e., comparison between common view and new proposal. (Modified from Ahissar & Hochstein, 2004.)

| | Comparison of old and new view of visual perception | | | | |
| | Common view | | New proposal | | |
Mechanism	*Site*	*Time*	*Site*	*Time*	*Evidence*
Gist of scene perception; basic level categorization	High	Late	High	Early	Rapid scene detection; illusory conjunctions
Subordinate categories	High	Late	Low	Late	High areas represent basic categories, no evidence for still higher areas
Focused attention	High	Late	Low	Late	Late attention effects in V1; "inattentional" blindness top-down guided
Feature search pop-out; illusory conjunctions	Low	Early	High	Early	High-level features and large j.n.d.; parallel search (spread attention)
Search for conjunctions and difficult discriminations	High	Late	Low	Late	Discrimination j.n.d. matches low-level fine resolution
Easy-condition perceptual learning	High	Late	High	Early	Rapid generalized learning

The basic rationale of relational measurement theory

Of particular interest here is Donald Laming's (1997) brief but useful account of David H. Krantz's (1972) and Roger N. Shepard's (1978, 1981a) early measurement theorizing. Remarkably, although Krantz's and Shepard's *relational* approach in psychophysical measurement theory was suggested quite a while ago, it has not notably changed mainstream psychophysics until today – probably since it was not based on a systematic and firm body of experimental evidence in both human and animal research. In fact, up until now the contents and methods of cognitive psychophysics rely mostly on traditional thinking, i.e., so far *relational psychophysics* has not been worked out systematically. At any rate, whereas classical sensory psychophysics is based mainly on the – illusory – assumption of absolute, i.e., invariant stimulus-response laws, the relation theory in cognitive psychophysics follows the general premise that, on principle, one and the same stimuli are perceived and judged very differently as a function of the variables provided by the total contextual situation at hand.

Remarks

As Shepard (1981a, p. 40) points out, his assumption has been that the resulting measurement scale, by the assigning of a subjective value to each single physical value, actually exists experimentally. In the same general vein, Krantz (1972) had his concept of a so-called "mapping" theory. Probably, the major difference between the two kinds of relational theorizing concerns the assumption of a missing versus existing scale unit. Furthermore, Shepard's idea has been that the primary psychophysical judgement concerns a sensation-perception *ratio* between a given physical stimulus pair. Conversely, Krantz presented his measurement theory at an abstract axiomatic level. Indeed, as Donald Laming notes, the preference of Shepard's over Krantz's mathematical reasoning may be perhaps ". . . [nothing] more than a matter of style and, from an *empirical* standpoint, [even] uninteresting" (Laming, 1997, p. 126; emphasis VS).

Above all, the reader should keep in mind that the various mathematical accounts as presented in this book are an attempt to suggest converging variants of a – still missing – *relation theory* in psychophysics (see below; see also chapters 2 and 3 and especially Appendix 2 and Appendix 3).

Multidimensional process scaling

Ronald M. Nosofsky (1992), in his provoking *Annual Review of Psychology* paper, has proposed a general process model of multidimensional *similarity* scaling as an extension of Shepard's (1987) universal exponential *law* of cognitive-similarity judgements. He claimed that such an advocated process model for psychophysical scaling ". . . could easily be incorporated in the connectionist-modeling domain [in order] to test the quantitative predictions of a given connectionist model of category learning" (Nosofsky, 1992, p. 49; see also Marr, 1982, Figure 6.11; Nosofsky, 1986, 1997). Nevertheless, despite the challenging character of Nosofky's theoretical approach in multidimensional human psychophysics, it has been silent on the still unsettled issues related to the so-called *separable-integral* information-processing concept in comparative developmental perception and psychophysics (for more see Shepard, 1981a, 1981b, 2001; see also Townsend & Pomerantz, 2004; Townsend & Spencer-Smith, 2004; Townsend & Wenger, 2004).

Relational psychophysics and cognitive neuroscience

The three-stage model of visual cognition, as outlined above (Figure 5.1), allows the notion of a ratio principle holding at each stage. In fact, it is meant here to be the basis of a general relational psychophysics and measurement theory (see also Kubovy & Gepshtein, 2003). This basic concept is in agreement with the following multimode distinction, as suggested elsewhere in line with more recent neuroanatomical and neurophysiological findings (Ehrenstein et al. 2003).

Probably, there exist three main kinds of information processing between the retina and the visual cortex, which are:

- afferent or feed-forward connections from the retina to the visual centres
- efferent or feedback connections from higher to lower cortical levels
- horizontal, long-range cortical connections.

The first mode is implied if one understands that sensory information processing relies mainly on *innate* conditions for the acquisition of visual experience behaviour. The second mode reflects a modifying influence of the visual input by perceptual synthesis. The third mode points to the findings of perceptual-cognitive memory and selective attention processing (top-down; see Table 5.1; see also Figure 2, p. 436 in Ehrenstein et al.'s 2003 article; furthermore see Bülthoff, Bülthoff, & Sinha, 1998; Walsh & Kulikowski, 1998).

Research examples: the three-stage model

Typical research examples for the present three-stage model are given here as follows:

Stage 1: Sensory adaptation and contrast

Already 20 years ago, John M. Allman and his colleagues reported their pioneering study on the relational basis of motion perception in cats (Allman, Miezin, & McGuiness, 1985; see also Allman, 1999). It was shown that MT neurons in the cat's visual cortex were sensitive not only to the direction of motion of the respective target objects but also to the movement of the background (surrounding context). When the screen was filled with a background of coherently moving dots, it was found "that the direction of motion of the dots moving entirely outside the classical [target] receptive field had a powerful and specific effect on the responses to stimuli within the classical receptive field. Thus the response of the neurons was jointly dependent on stimuli within the classical field and outside it" (Allman, 1999, pp. 136–137; see also Albright, Croner, Duncan, & Stoner, 2003; Engel & Singer, 2001; Engel et al. 2001; Singer, 1999, 2004; von der Heydt, Zhou & Friedman, 2003).

Stage 2: Perceptual frame-of-reference phenomena

One typical candidate for this stage, with its neurobiological basis of relational perception, is the phenomenon of the *Kanizsa* illusional-pattern perception in both animal and human research, as described above (chapter 1, Figure 1.2). The neurobiological basis of this classical gestalt phenomenon (*perceptual synthesis*) has been successfully investigated by Rüdiger von der Heydt, now at Johns Hopkins University, USA (c.f., Gauthier & Palmeri, 2002; Gilbert & Wiesel, 1990; Peterhans & von der Heydt, 1991; von der Heydt & Peterhans, 1989; see also Ehrenstein et al., 2003; Nakayama, Shimojo, & Ramachandran, 1990; Nieder, 2002; Spillmann & Ehrenstein, 2004; Tomasi, 2003). However, until today it is unclear if and to what extent other frame-of-reference effects can be also explained by von der Heydt's *early-process* account (Gerald M. Westheimer, personal communication, May 1998; see Westheimer, 1999).

Stage 3: Memory and cognitive decision making

This stage is neurobiologically the least understood, due to the intriguing bottom-up and top-down interactions of the neurophysiological processes at the stages 2 and 3 (e.g., Walsh & Kulikowski, 1998; pp. 1ff; see Figure 5.1 *fair* question). Nevertheless, in human psychophysics the massive amount of stage 3 related research into the memory and decision making plus instructional-set processes is still rather vague (piecemeal) but thought provoking and noteworthy. This is also true for the neuro-network approach as presented below (see also Haubensak & Petzold, 2002; Mori, 1998; Mori & Ward, 1995; Petrusic, 2001, 2003; Petzold & Haubensak, 2004; Ward, 1973, 1979, 1987, 1992; furthermore, see Ghirlanda & Enquist, 2003; Petrov & Anderson, 2005; Wedell, 2004).

In light of the arguable status of today's neuroscientific explanatory basis of the higher order perceptual processing, the next paragraph contains a brief account of a neuro-network model of perceptual learning and memory phenomena (see Ehrenstein et al., 2003; Jacobs, 2003; see also Johnson & Munakata, 2005; Lee, 2003; Nieder, 2002; Pasternak & Greenlee, 2005).

Toward a neural-network model of perceptual learning

The assumed nonlinear dynamics of cognitive processes and perceptual learning should be of considerable interest for the proper modelling of contextual effects in comparative psychophysics. The attempt to better understand, say, the baby chick's and the human infant's psychophysical performing and its neurobiological functioning is here at stake (for instance, see Grossberg's *adaptive resonance theory* as a general account of the neural-network approach; e.g., Grossberg, 1999, 2000).

A neural-network model

The following application and extension of the neural-network model suggested by Mark H. Johnson, London, for the baby chick and its transposition behaviour shows potential. Johnson (1999, 2005) proposed a two-process theory for the infant chick's brain circuitry during the imprinting phase, resting on the assumption of a basic linkage between imprinting and perceptual learning during infancy. His theory starts with the consideration of the functioning of a subcortical visual-pathway unit on the one hand, and a forebrain (cortical) module in the so-called *intermediate medial hyperstriatum ventrale (IMHV)* on the other. This idea forms the basis of a connectionist model that consists of different layers with a detailed architecture designed around the neuroanatomical connection of the aforementioned two brain areas (Figures. 5.2 and 5.3).

With his neural-network model, Mark H. Johnson (1999, 2005; O'Reilly & Johnson, 1994) has simulated some basic perceptual-learning phenomena associated with imprinting in the chick, especially with regard to the so-called *critical period*. However, even for the infant chick's brain and behaviour, the respective neurobiological and comparative psychophysical sets of data are far from being complete (e.g., Honey & Bolhuis, 1997; Honey, Horn, & Bateson, 1992). It remains to be seen in future research if, and to what extent, this model might be useful not only to simulate the chick's most elementary responses but also to allow some truly novel predictions, such as those concerning transposition and different kinds of psychophysical context effects during the post-discrimination phase of chickens as well as of other species.

Further research issues: nonlinear psychophysics

The neural-network approach should be specified by *mathematical model building*, as described more specifically in the end of this book (see Appendix 2; see also Appendix 3).

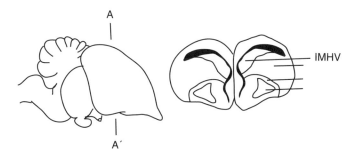

Figure 5.2 Neuro-anatomy and neurobiological functioning of the infant chicken's perceptual behaviour during imprinting and learning. *Left*: the vertical lines A' indicate the plane of the coronal section outline (*right*) of the chick brain (IMHV means the intermediate and medial part of the hyperstriatum ventrale). This biopsychological scheme of Mark H. Johnson (1999, 2005) may become a fruitful comparative model of the ontogenesis of perception in different species. (Adapted from Johnson, 1999, 2005.)

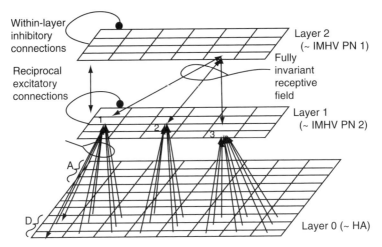

Figure 5.3 The detailed architecture of the IMHV (see Figure 5.2) designed around the anatomical connectivity of IMHV and its primary input area, i.e., the hyperstriatum accessorium (HA). The model is based on a set of layers, each of which has lateral inhibition within them. The "input" layer of the network, layer 0, represents HA, which projects to one subpopulation of IMHV cells (so-called Type 1 PNs). This is layer 1 of the IMHV component of the model. Note that the laminar distinction in the model between these two component cells. IMHV is not intended to suggest that the cells are arranged as such in the IMHV itself, but rather serves to reflect the functional distinction between the two types of PN cells. The axons from the Type 1 neurons project to the Type 2 projection neurons, as well as onto the local inhibitory neurons. This composes the second layer of the model's IMHV component. (Adapted from Johnson, 1999: Figure 9.2.)

Nonlinear psychophysics of perceptual magnitudes

The model advanced here – and still open for debate – has been developed more fully elsewhere by Gregson (e.g., 1988) as a nonlinear approach to psychophysics, deliberately choosing to avoid the traditional linear models with a residual, stochastic independent noise component. This nonlinear approach has some properties and formal advantages which may enable apparently diverse and unrelated phenomena in psychophysics to be treated within a single framework (c.f. also Gregson, 1992, chapter 4).

The present account is only concerned with temporary shifts in the psychophysical *S-R* function, which can variously be approximated by a *cumulative normal ogive* (*CNO*) or sometimes better by a cubic polynomial over the stimulus range used and with the reported tendency of dynamic systems to restabilize in the neighbourhood of a maximum entropy form of the *S-R* function. The following general difference equation represents the action of a massive neural array, with feedback, and excitation level Y_j at time j:

$$Y_{j+1} = -a\_(Y_j \pm e)(Y_j - 1), \tag{5.1}$$

where j is in discrete time, a is a real, e is an imaginary compoment, and $Y_j \pm e$ is a complex conjugate pair (see Gregson, 1988, for a lengthy treatment of the dynamic meaning of this model). We study here the behaviour of the real part of Y after the recursive process in Equation (5.1) has been through n steps (i.e. $j = 1,2,\ldots.n$).

A note on the nonlinear equation 5.1

Note that Equation (5.1) is only one of a wide class of difference equations that can exhibit alternative modes of functioning. As we increase the value of a single parameter in the system (usually a, here) at low values of the parameter the output always converges to the same limit in Y. At medium values it goes into cyclic behaviour which can in turn exhibit jumps in its periodicity (called *bifurcations*), doubling and redoubling, and with yet further increases in the value of a the system moves into aperiodic chaos, governed in its dynamics by what is called a strange attractor (Gregson, 1988). It has to be emphasized that all this behaviour is deterministic; that is there are no random processes within the system, though the input from the environment can be random, and for illustration in simulations we usually would make it so.

In the model the general nonlinear Equation 5.1 is made to be the representation of a recursive loop which is in turn incorporated within a minimum complexity system. This does not represent the neuro-anatomy of feedback in higher sensory or perceptual-cognitive processes, but is rather a model of its simplest possible equivalent mode of operation in a systems-theory approach. That is essentially all there is. The model's loop components can be repeated in series, that is to say *cascaded*, as shown schematically in Figure 5.4.

Peculiarities of equation 5.1

Some subtleties arise from the way that the input signals U (the magnitudes of the stimuli in physical units) from the environment are fed into the loop, via a link W. Instead of the U going directly onto the loop variable Y, which is the simplest way to think of transmitting signals into a loop, the loop variable is autonomous and has its own resting level Y_0. Instead the inputs map onto the loop parameters a and e, or simply onto a, and a and e are adjustable within limits. So, in effect, the loop flips ("dances") between alternative modes of chaos. There is no random noise here at all, but when the inner loop is in a chaotic phase then to an external observer the output looks random and can only be distinguished from a random series by time-series analysis. One problem with the *loop hypothesis* of Gregson (1988) is that it is proposed ad hoc to explain the variability of responses. After all, no such loop has been found physiologically, and several other formulations

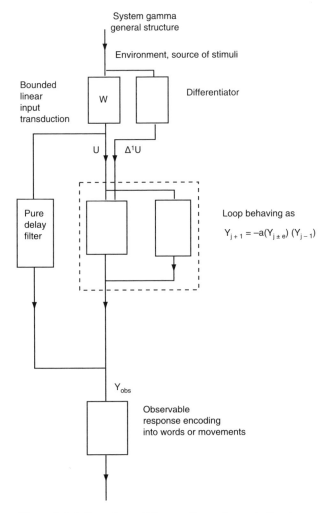

Figure 5.4 A flow chart of the nonlinear dynamic "system gamma general structure", as suggested for the dynamic modelling of psychophysical
transposition "shifts" in comparative perception. (Adapted from
Gregson & Sarris, 1985; see Appendix 2.)

are possible (Ward, 1979; Lawrence M. Ward, personal communication,
April 2005).

Nonlinear dynamic system and transposition

Nonlinear dynamic equations have the property that very small changes in a
parameter can lead later to very divergent paths being traced out by the
system; small internal changes do not only lead to small external consequences. It is interesting to consider how this system would behave if we put

it into a hypothetical transposition experiment. The changes in stimulus ranges are representable by remarkable changes in the way that U is mapped onto the variable a, and there are necessarily, even in a model as simple as this, alternative ways in which changes in *frame of reference* might influence changes in the S-R function.

An important feature, which might suggest that displacements ("shifts") are being mapped into a far-from-equilibrium region of the system parameter space, is the observable *abruptness* of changes from one form of S-R function to another. Various data as obtained in Sarris's psychophysics lab appear to "jump" in the relative frequency of responses in a two-category response task, i.e., they appear to occur very abruptly and then to persist in a stable form. Typically, the total duration of such experiments is not sufficient to expect to observe restabilization. If the data are pooled over sessions and subjects, then a gradual transition of PSIs is suggested to be occurring, but this is misleading because the gradualness appears to arise from the delay having a distribution in time across subjects.

Indeed, the abruptness of shifts within the responses of one subject is particularly significant from a nonlinear systems perspective. It appears that nonlinear biological systems which are dissipative not only exhibit the qualitative features of frame-of-reference experiments, but must do so. These features are characteristic of biological self-regulating systems, and it is clear that neurophysiologically what is mediating the behaviour in a frame-of-reference experiment is a massive aggregation of biological elements that can function in synchrony, are subject to quasi-random inputs, and can be described in some of their overall dynamic input-output relations by the Gregson's system model, codified here in Equation 5.1. While that system model implies that the detection and difference thresholds are coupled, the frame-of-reference results say nothing about thresholds, but simply predict that a shift in the stimulus range induces the observer to operate temporarily in a different part of the S-R function. It should be noted that such results may be quite different from one experiment to another or from one species to another (e.g., Wilson, Mackintosh, & Boakes, 1985).

In some cases a shift in the stimulus range induces transposition, in other cases if the shift is greater the responses become *absolute*. Furthermore, depending on the method used, some species may not show transposition at all. This diversity of behaviour might perhaps be accounted for by postulating that a small shift in the range of U induces a compensatory shift in e within the observer which holds the S-R form about the same. A large shift in U is too great for the internal dynamics to compensate for, and a consequent shift of the S-R function is induced. The problem with this sort of explanation is to define for a given observer what is a "small" and what is a "large" shift in U. So, varying e would produce an analogue of the frame-of-reference effects, whereas varying U onto a would produce, for fixed e, the Crozier invariances; i.e., threshold and S-R transform changes need to be represented in Γ in quite different regions of the system's parameter space.

Remarks

A much more specified theory-directed and model-testing oriented approach would be most desirable, along with more comparative psychophysics experimentation, namely that present and future studies in relational psychophysics should also be guided by a multi-stage process-oriented research strategy for the further development and experimental analysis of animal/human models and theories of perception (see chapter 6; see also Nosofsky, 1986, 1992, 1997). For a lengthy treatment of the above nonlinear model approach to frame-of-reference transposition shifts see Gregson's book, in which the application of Sarris and his co-workers' earlier sets of chick data are described (Gregson, 1988, chapter 12; see also Gregson, 1992, chapter 4). Another useful monograph on nonlinear dynamic model building is by Lawrence M. Ward (2002). Furthermore, the *fuzzy logic* model approach for this comparative psychophysics conception is of interest, although beyond the scope of this book. Note that already Ward (1979) used the *fuzzy set* concept in his theory of magnitude estimation and cross-modality matching (there the categories are conceptualized as fuzzy sets and so are the representations of stimuli). For a brief overview see Zadeh (2001) or Yager (2003; see also Brainerd & Reyna, 1990, 1993; Enquist & Ghirlanda, 2005).

Summary and conclusions

This theory-oriented chapter on comparative perception and psychophysics presents a multiple-stage model of the putative intertwined processes involved in the developing human and animal mind (Figure 5.1). Especially emphasized are the cognitive aspects of this *three-stage model*, despite the fact that its heuristic value is still controversial (bottom-up versus top-down processing). Nevertheless, even though it still lacks experimental rigour, the present multiple-stage approach is held to be the fundament of relational psychophysics for the sake of further substantiation of animal and human research, in line also with the modern cognitive neuroscience work (e.g., Johnson, 1999, 2005; see also Gazzaniga, 2000, 2004). In light of the author's own research, the importance of a stepwise formulation and testing of specific mathematical models is desirable for the further foundation of a dynamic nonlinear relational psychophysics. All in all, this chapter forms the basis for the concluding discussion of this book (see also Appendix 2 & Appendix 3).

6 General discussion and conclusions

Continuing with animal consciousness, why stop at mice or, indeed, at mammals? . . . Do we really know that the cerebral cortex and its satellites are necessary for perceptual consciousness? Why not squids? Or bees? Endowed with one million neurons, bees can perform complicated actions, including amazing feats of visual pattern matching . . . Maybe even fruitflies are conscious, to a very limited extent. Today we just don't know.

(Koch, 2004, p. 320)

Introduction

In this final chapter on comparative cognitive psychophysics an attempt is made to expand relational psychophysics to other fields of visual perception, for example, to the principles of *perceptual constancy* and *perceptual memory*. After all, where do we go from here, leaving aside for a while the enduring question of animal awareness and consciousness in comparative perception and psychophysics for the next research generations to come (human versus animal *consciousness*)?

Indeed, future experimentation should also be done in the light of other research domains, thus trying to overcome the narrowness of the past research agenda in psychophysics, despite the historical successes which psychophysics has achieved with regard to its quantitative methodology, experimental law building, and mathematical theorizing during the past 150 years (c.f. the *testing-the-limits* approach: e.g., Heidelberger, 2004; Kaernbach et al., 2004). After all, one of the principal questions being raised here has been and remains: *Which concrete lines of future work should be followed; and will, for instance, a neural-network approach in comparative-developmental psychophysics support the respective demands?*

Major questions raised in this book

First, the answers to the major questions dealt with in chapters 1 through 5 are briefly summarized as follows:

- *Chapter 1: Relational perception and epistemology*. It is held here that there are viable research bridges between modern (neo-) gestalt approaches and perceptual-cognitive psychophysics, notwithstanding the fact that certain enduring epistemological issues have not – or cannot, on principle – be resolved (e.g., see the *mind–body* problem: see Figure 1.1).
- *Chapter 2: Frame-of-reference* (FR) *models in psychophysics*. The different FR models, including the SC model with the *Sarris effect* (Link, 2004; Parducci, 2004), although limited in their explanatory accounts, have formed the basis of a viable research approach, especially when considered from a comparative and developmental perceptual-cognitive perspective (Figure 6.1).
- *Chapter 3: Behavioural psychophysics and relational perception*. A systematic behavioural approach in FR psychophysics has allowed the study of the classical *transposition* phenomenon comparatively, both with humans and animals, thus leading to the predicted perceptual-cognitive "shift" effects (see also the *Sarris effect*). The major findings as described above should also be seen from the earlier gestalt ("relational") perspective, however now based on a close linkage between modern psychophysical methodology and perceptual-memory research.
- *Chapter 4: Developmental psychophysics*. The foregoing main ideas and findings, as presented in chapter 3, have been successfully extended to comparative age-related work with both humans and birds (cross-species comparison). One of the major results was the experimental evidence for the absolute and relational perceptual memory processing already in the infant chicken (*awakening cognition*). It is clear, however, that much more parametric and measurement-oriented research in this area of developmental psychophysics is required, especially with regard to the paradigmatic extensions to human and other animal infants.
- *Chapter 5: New perspectives in perceptual-cognitive psychophysics*. In this theory-oriented part it was argued that present and future research should be directed by a *multiple-stage model*, thus finding both the differences and the links between the absolute and relational factors governing the different sensory and perceptual-cognitive processes in the various animal species. Such an approach should include the major aspects of cognitive neuroscience and nonlinear psychophysics (*mathematical model building*: see Appendix 2 & Appendix 3).

In the following sections of this concluding chapter some of today's most challenging questions are extended to future research work.

Perceptual constancy and memory in psychophysics

Recently, FR research in psychophysics has included the systematic study of some of the fundamental *short-term* and *long-term* memory processes involved in psychophysical behaviour, in accordance with mathematical

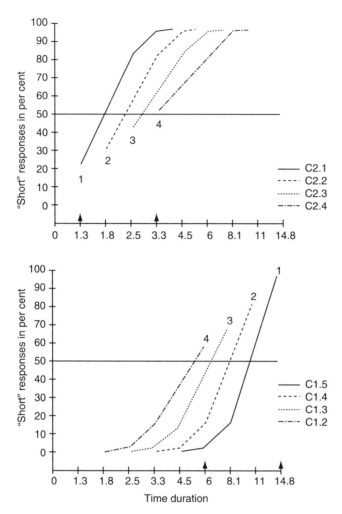

Figure 6.1 Gradual increase and disappearance of psychophysical context effects with moderate versus extreme test-series stimuli (the *Sarris effect*). Note that the predictive context-dependent trends (i.e., transposition shifts) in this graph of postgeneralization testing have been described and illustrated in this book, both theoretically and experimentally (see chapter 3). (Adapted from Cangöz, 1999.)

model building (e.g., DeCarlo, 2003; Petrov & Anderson, 2005; Petzold & Haubensak, 2004; see also Rescorla, 2003; Wagner, 2003). In this context, the following general question is raised and needs to be answered specifically in future work: *Are there feasible links between relational psychophysics and the perceptual constancy phenomena?*

Perceptual constancy and memory

It is suggested here that the *frame-of-reference* (*FR*) notion might be most fruitfully addressed in light of the comparative and developmental perspectives of perceptual constancy (cognitive stability) and perceptual memory (Gregory, 2003, p. 465; see also Karmiloff-Smith, 1992; Walsh & Kulikowski, 1998). Indeed, as a consequence of past research, the paradigmatic analysis of perceptual memory processes should become obligatory in cross-species and developmental psychophysics.

Surely, the context findings as reported in this book must not be dismissed as mere biases such as sensory-perceptual "distortions", memory and learning "anomalies", or dubious judgemental "response sets". On the contrary, it appears that the above-stated context and transposition effects reflect some basic perceptual-cognitive and perceptual memory phenomena that are common at least to the vertebrate species like chickens, cats, apes and humans – notwithstanding the problem of how to disentangle the processes involved at the behavioural and neurobiological levels (see Figure 5.1; see Walsh & Kulikowski, 1998 on perceptual constancy, especially Neumeyer's overview, 1998; see also Neumeyer, 1991). Note that the paradigmatic analysis of short- and long-term memory processes must be based on a sound developmental-biopsychological methodology, including the cross-sectional and longitudinal research approach (see Bateson's, 1991, see here Figure 6.2).

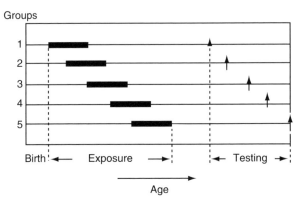

Figure 6.2 A general cross-sectional and longitudinal research design in comparative perception and psychophysics with infant animals. The scheme illustrates that, for instance, five different groups of subjects (e.g., chickens, cats, monkeys) are exposed to an imprinting object since birth, starting at different ages (the imprinting object is denoted by the thick horizontal bars; the onset of subsequent testing is illustrated by the vertical arrows). The duration of stimulus exposure is the same for all groups. If the age of testing is kept constant, the time elapsed from the end of exposure to testing varies accordingly. (Adapted from Bateson, 1991.)

The stimulus-range issue in comparative psychophysics

The influence of the *range* constitutes a challenging problem for psychophysics, both theoretically and practically. One major aspect of relational psychophysics is related to the general problem of context effects on psychophysical scaling and measurement. Some types of contextual shifts due to the stimulus-range and stimulus-asymmetry ("anchoring" and "similarity") are particularly important (see chapters 2, 3, 4).

To be sure, a *range finder*, as used for instance in photography and engineering, is an optical measurement device to determine the exact distance (range) between the camera and the object to be photographed. This physical instrument is commonly used by the military to precisely read the distance between a weapon and a target. In psychophysics, however, the range, by analogy, refers to the lowest and highest score along a physical scale over which a particular sensory system functions. In stark contrast to the case of engineering, however the measurements taken in psychophysics are known to be *context* dependent (e.g., Parker & Schneider 1994; Teghtsoonian & Teghtsoonian, 2003). According to R. Duncan Luce's (2004) recent observation it may be of interest to learn that the context measurement theory of David R. Krantz (1972; see also Shepard, 1978, 1981a, 1981b) has been unduly ignored until today.

Developmental and animal psychophysics

By way of a brief summary, as an alternative and/or addition to the verbal rating method, comparative psychophysics is concerned with the use of *behavioural methods*, in line with the following Examples A and B taken from Sarris's developmental and animal research:

Example A: Developmental psychophysics

According to the general behavioural training-context test paradigm used, age-related data were gathered with human participants for several modalities (e.g., size and duration judgements). As an illustration, some empirical data stemming from size judgements made by kindergarten children have been provided as shown in detail elsewhere (chapter 3). Clearly, these contextual shifts are in line with the overall prediction of lawful psychophysical "relativity" effects that are due to the variable test-series asymmetry. They reflect the relative nature of psychophysical responding: one and the same physical stimulus was responded to as either "large" or "small," depending on the respective test conditions used. These asymmetry context findings illustrate fundamental range-extension effects. Notably the more extreme asymmetry conditions lead to fewer context shifts for children than for adults.

Example B: Animal psychophysics

In accordance with the general behavioural psychophysics context-test paradigm used, some systematic comparative investigations with chickens were conducted. In a series of experiments carried out with different groups of young hens, the classic successive choice-discrimination procedure was employed along with a post-discrimination technique that contained the variable contextual ("asymmetry") test series. The chickens were tested with different context series of mostly *new* cube sizes, i.e., with either increasingly smaller or larger volumes. As the main result, the context-induced test series *Point of Subjective Indifference* (*PSI*) shifts were very similar to those observed with the human participants (see chapter 3). However, the contextual PSI-test shifting of the chickens occurred at a much slower rate than observed with the human subjects – an important comparative finding, due to the different perceptual memory processes involved for the birds and the humans. In addition to these findings, the ontogenetic development of the infant chicken's relative versus absolute context-dependent behaviour was also studied systematically (see chapter 4).

Relational perception and psychophysics

Up until now the contents and methods of psychophysics rely mostly on traditional thinking; i.e., *relational psychophysics* has not been worked out systematically. Whereas classical sensory psychophysics is based mainly on the (illusory) assumption of absolute, i.e., invariant stimulus-response laws, the relation theory in psychophysics follows the general premise that, on principle, a given stimulus object is perceived and judged very differently as a function of the variables provided by the total contextual situation at hand.

Additional unresolved questions

Nevertheless, there have been and still are many additional questions involved, which are in need of further clarification (e.g., Petrov & Anderson, 2005, Teghtsoonian & Teghtsoonian, 2003). To begin with, more systematic experimental work has to disentangle the range and the asymmetry factors implied in developmental and comparative research. In addition, there are several major, and many more subtle, aspects of the sensory-perceptual and cognitive-judgemental processes involved. Indeed, some time ago Allen Parducci (1982) claimed that "*there is no psychophysical law!*" readily to be found on a firm empirical basis. On the other hand, the more recent research trend on short-term and long-term memory related to the psychophysical frame-of-reference processing seems promising (e.g., DeCarlo, 2003; Petrov & Anderson, 2005; Petzold & Haubensak, 2004). It may well be that further inquiry will support Martha and Robert Teghtsoonian's (2003) more optimistic conclusion that there exist some fruitful solutions to the *lawfulness* perplexity in human psychophysics (see also N. H. Anderson, 1983, 2001; Norman H. Anderson, personal communication, November 2004).

Toward a comparative-developmental theory in psychophysics

In a special section on the relativity of perception, Kenneth H. Norwich (1993) points to the philosopher George Berkeley's (1710) early emphasis on the relational character of all human perception and cognition, foreshadowing the epistemological basis of psychophysics and perception in the nineteenth and twentieth centuries. Whatever the future of psychophysics will bring during the next decades, it seems clear that the search for an advanced knowledge of quantitative laws in sensation, perception and cognition will still be based on Berkeley's general philosophical credo (*perceptual relativity*).

Some remaining challenges to psychophysics

Looking back to the last ten or twenty years in human and animal research, one may be pleased – but also become easily overwhelmed at the same time – by the wealth of different topics investigated under the umbrella term of psychophysics. As in much of psychology as a whole, there is a great freedom today concerning what is, or should be, important research in psychophysics, clearly beyond the Weber-Fechner issues of sensation (e.g., Baird, 1997; Lockhead, 1992, 2004; Ward, 2003).

Signal-detection theory (SDT) and psychophysics

Nowadays, SDT with its conceptual and methodological impact is no longer a revolutionary approach to psychophysics as suggested half a century ago with its claim to "disentangle" sensory and decision processes in perception and psychophysics (e.g., Green & Swets, 1966; Swets, 1996). Rather, there remains the challenging problem of *how* to disentangle the basic sensory, perceptual and cognitive processes involved in the human and animal species' psychophysical behaviour (e.g., Heinemann & Chase, 1990; Tyler & Chen, 2000; see also Lu & Dosher, 2000; Lu, Jeon, & Dosher, 2004).

Uni- and multidimensional psychophysics

The longstanding issue of uni- and multidimensional psychophysics needs ongoing theoretical and experimental work. Especially, what we need to understand more fully is the problem of *separable* and/or *integral* dimensions in multiple-context perception and psychophysics (e.g., Townsend & Spencer-Smith, 2004; see also chapter 5).

Remarks

Clearly, there is important expertise and competence of the specialists in the subfields of interest; on the other side, there has been – and still is – a disturbing lack of experimental and theoretical coherence between the different areas of psychophysics. Indeed, the methods and paradigms used in current research are impressive for the uniquely trained specialist. However, they may hardly be understood or appreciated by the psychophysicist belonging to another special field. Surely, without doubt there is the need for specialized work, but at the same time – more than ever – there is a logistic challenge concerning effective research communication among the scholars of modern psychophysical research.

At this point, special attention may be paid to a recent book with the somewhat provocative title *Psychophysics Beyond Sensation: Laws and Invariants of Human Cognition*, which includes challenging "Guest Editorials" by leading psychophysicists (Kaernbach, et al., 2004). This collective work contains many examples which point to the essence of this author's major claims on developmental and comparative psychophysics. Arguably, some of the related articles of that book might also – nay, should – be evaluated in the context of a most recent publication by Mark H. Johnson and Yuko Munakata (2005), as shown below.

Comparative psychophysics and nonlinear dynamics

In line with the volumes edited by Mark A. Berkley and William C. Stebbins (1990) *Comparative Perception: Basic Mechanisms* and, more specifically, by R. J. Andrew (1991) *Neural and Behavioural Plasticity: The Use of the Domestic Chick as a Model*, some major lines of today's and perhaps also tomorrow's psychophysics with other animals are highlighted. This combines animal perception with human developmental psychophysics research, at least in principle (see also Atkinson, 2000; Rogers, 1995). There have been in the past several *nonlinear* dynamic approaches in psychophysics (see chapter 5; Appendix 2 & Appendix 3). The time has come to try and combine such research approaches with neuroinformatics and robotics, on the basis of developmental comparative experimentation (for instance, see Braitenberg, 1984; Erlhagen, 2003; Erlhagen & Jahnke, 2004; Erlhagen & Schöner, 2002; Ghirlanda, 2002; Ghirlanda & Enquist, 2003; Ward, 2002).

The assumed nonlinear dynamics of the cognitive processes in *perceptual learning* is of considerable interest for the proper modelling of contextual effects in comparative psychophysics (see also modern research methodology, for instance *transcranial magnetic stimulation, TMS*: e.g., Cowey & Walsh, 2001; Pasternak & Greenlee, 2005; Walsh & Pascual-Leone, 2003). Although such a far-reaching approach might be considered premature given the debatable state of cross-species experimental evidence, the attempt to better understand, say, the infant chick's and other creatures' psychophysical performance is probably worthwhile. As already suggested (chapter 5), the application and further extension of a neuro-network approach for the chick's brain circuitry during the imprinting and perceptual learning phase may be a good starting point for future breakthrough studies (see Figure 6.2). Indeed, the psychophysical analysis of such perceptual-cognitive processes, in light of our frame-of-reference and transposition paradigm, has much to offer in contributing to the growing field of comparative perception, beyond the low-level stage of sensation (see also Humphreys, 2003; Jacobs, 2003; Lee, 2003).

Future research directions – an evolutionary perspective

An example of a hypothetical biopsychological (*cross-species*) extension of our present research agenda is developed and described by Richard G. M. Morris (1994; Figure 11, p. 163; see here Figure 6.3). This psychopharmacological paradigm takes the factual high *interindividual variability* – "poor" versus "good" learners – of perceptual performance into account, suggesting a substantial improvement of the animal's overall learning and memory capacity under certain psychopharmacological drug conditions. The diagram in Morris's original figure indicates stark neurophysiological plasticity differences in a so-called saturation experiment with different animals: the "good" learners" in contrast to the "poor learners" may be those that show relatively

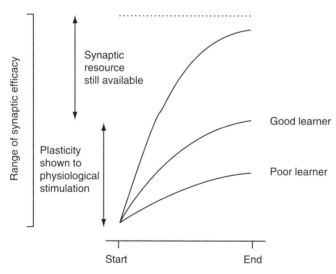

Figure 6.3 A biopsychological ("cross-species") example for some future research: psychopharmacological and psychophysical paradigms combined. The diagram illustrates the variable "plasticity"/"synaptic resource" capacity from start to end for the "poor" versus "good" learners. Note that the assumed variable capacity may be systematically altered by the given pharmaceutical substance. (Adapted from Morris, 1994.)

greater *long-term potentiation* (*LTP*) effects until they reach the asymptote (see also Chun, 2005; Ranganath & Blumenfeld, 2005; Ryan & Cohen, 2004).

Clear progress has been made in cognitive psychophysics, but alas many controversial issues and open questions remain, implying challenging ideas for the near or not too distant future of comparative research (for instance, see Spillmann, 2005; Tarr & Bülthoff, 1998; Watt & Phillips, 2005):

1   What are the measurable (psychophysical) processes involved in perceptual organization, or more specifically: Is perceptual synthesis, e.g., relational cognition, an "early" and/or a "late" process?
2   What are the necessary and sufficient input ("stimulus") factors that evoke and/or trigger the processes of perceptual organization, in humans and other animals?
3   What are the neurobiological mechanisms underlying perceptual processes of different kinds in infant and adult creatures (e.g., von Hofsten, 2002, 2004; see also Ranganath & D'Esposito, 2005)?

Trends in cognitive sciences: special issue (2005)

In the *Special Issue: Developmental Cognitive Neuroscience*, recently edited by Mark H. Johnson and Yuko Munakata (2005), the compelling question is asked how evidence from the cognitive neurosciences has contributed to the current state of knowledge about cognitive development and its future research activities. Some of their major issues are of special interest here.

Species comparative studies (J.-C. Gomez, 2005)

The comparative investigation of human and animal cognitive development is demandatory, on the basis of similar conceptual frameworks and experimental methodologies. The past findings for different species call for an integration of current competing accounts of age-specific cognitive changes. Two examples of the main questions for future research are (Gomez, 2005, Box 4, p. 123):

•   Can infant humans and monkeys/apes pass looking-time tests, and other behavioural tasks of object permanence before manual search tests?
•   Do symbol training and human-like rearing affect cognitively by the developmental outcomes for different species alike?

Methodological challenges for human infant research (R. M. Aslin & J. Fiser, 2005)

Different methodological issues in infant learning and cognition are discussed including the intriguing behavioural measurement methodology. It is suggested that future progress in researching the infant cognitive development will also benefit from psychophysical paradigms that are closer (akin) to those used with human adults. Three examples of the major questions for future research are (Aslin & Fiser, 2005, Box 4, p. 97):

- Which are the age-specific limits on the amount of perceptual-cognitive information infants can take in "at a glance", and can such limits be changed by suitable pretraining?
- How detailed is the infant's cognitive representation of the given stimulus "environment" and how can the age-specific infant's representation be improved?
- Which are the higher cortical areas and how do they develop during the age-specific cognitive changes?

Connectionist models of cognitive development (J. L. Elman, 2005)

The advances in developmental neuroscience have also presented new challenges for the connectionist modellers, for instance, as to how the age-specific knowledge gains may be represented. Two examples of the main questions for future research are (Elman, 2005, Box 1, p. 116):

- *Multi-tasking*: whereas most computational models focus on single behaviours, it is also important to investigate how the developing child's behaviour in one domain interacts with behaviour in another one.
- *Time-related changes*: obviously most complex behaviours are the result of *"cascading"* processes (see here chapter 5) that depend on earlier developmental stages; the modelling of the respective developmental interactions over time is an urgent issue.

Evolutionary perception and psychophysics

A general scheme of a *perceptual-motor loop* in comparative (cross-species) biopsychology is shown here to emphasize the basic evolutionary impacts of developmental psychophysics (see Figure 6.4; see also Beniuc, 1932, 1933; Brecher, 1933; Gould, 2002; von Uexküll, 1934/1957; on cross-species perceptual relativity).

Miscellaneous issues: transposition, numerosity, transitivity

Furthermore, consider the multi-stage comparative psychophysics of transposition and *numerosity* in different species – say, birds, mice, gerbils, cats, primates. After all, both humans and animals have been shown to be sensitive to relational numerosity of perceptual objects (e.g., Beran, 2004; Beran & Beran, 2004; Dehaene, 2003; Emmerton, 2001; Feigenson, Dehaene, & Spelke, 2004). In addition, the comparative research on transposition and *transitivity* should be systematically revived and extended in light of a

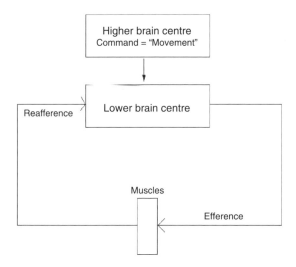

Figure 6.4 Schematic diagram: an evolutionary research perspective for the future study of comparative perception and psychophysics. The diagram illustrates the "lower" and "higher" centres and their interplay according to the general efference/reafference principle. (Modified from Dittrich & Lea, 2001.)

cognitive psychophysics paradigm (e.g., see DeLillo, Floreano, & Antinucci, 2001; Klix, 2003; Lazareva, Smirnova, Bacozkaja, Zorina, Rayevsky, & Wasserman, 2005; Siemann & Delius, 1998; see also Plotkin, 2004; Zentall & Wasserman, 2005).

Outstanding question

Are there substantial connections between transposition, a perceptual-cognitive phenomenon and transitivity, a higher order cognitive concept? Probably there is some sense of transposition in the so-called "transitive inference" tasks. It may well be that there is an associative mechanism which enables humans and other primates – perhaps even some lower species – to build up "chains" across certain paired cognitive items, not dependent on subjects' awareness of the temporal item relationships. But this putative possibility is open for discussion and is in need of convincing empirical support (e.g., Howard, 2004; Howard, Fotedar, Datey, & Hasselmo, 2005; Zayan & Vauclair, 1998; Marc W. Howard, Syracuse University, USA, personal communication, September 2005).

Summary and conclusions

In this concluding chapter the general frame-of-reference (FR) paradigm in psychophysics has been discussed and extended in relation to some demanding comparative issues of perceptual constancy and memory, including cross-sectional and longitudinal research methodology. Instead of a refinement of a – still lacking – comparative developmental theory of relational psychophysics, some major questions for the future of comparative psychophysics have been raised here. Finally, an attempt has been made to relate some of the suggested research directions also to an evolutionary perspective (*awakening cognition*). Despite enormous accomplishments made in the areas of comparative-developmental psychophysics over the last two or three decades, undoubtedly much more integrative biopsychological and neuro-network research needs to be done, especially on relational psychophysics:

> It would really be good to see cortical physiology – including whole-brain imaging approaches – go beyond the butterfly collection stage. We need to begin to address the real questions about how the brain solves the tremendously difficult problems of perception and thinking, the visual recognition of objects for example.
>
> (Poggio, 2004, p. 986)

Appendix 1
Apparatus for animal psychophysics

The equipment for the psychophysical work done with chickens, as described in chapter 3 of this monograph, consisted of a computer-controlled apparatus which permitted the successive presentation of different sized plus different coloured cubes (Figure A1.1, with two schematic views A and B).

The training and test sessions took place Monday through Friday, with two identical apparatuses working in parallel. Usually, the chickens were kept in individual cages overnight, but were allowed to stay in a group for at least four to six hours per day (Figure A1.2). The experiments were planned and conducted according to the ethical standards for animal treatment (*APA standards*; see also Engelmann, 1984). In order to help ensure these standards, at least once a year the housing and procedures were visited and checked by a minister's officer (*veterinary doctor*).

Apparatus

The computer-controlled apparatus permitted the successive presentation of three-dimensional objects (cubes). It consisted of a training and test box and a waiting compartment divided by an automatically controlled gliding door (Figure A1.1, *top*). The cubes were presented, one by one, in front of a $60 \times 60 \times 60$ cm wall on which two pecking keys and two food magazines were fastened, one to the left and the other to the right of the stimulus object. The objects were placed underneath the test box, each on an individual plate, located on a rotatable wheel (diameter 165 cm). A motor turned the wheel to the correct position; then the plate with the appropriate object was lifted hydraulically into the opening in the floor of the test box (see Figure A1.1, *bottom*).

Stimulus materials

The stimuli were red cubes differing in volume in equal logarithmic steps. All subjects were trained with the same pair of training stimuli (TS), a 215 ccm and a 608 ccm cube, but tested with three different test series. Table A1.1 shows the physical measurements of the main training and test stimuli. The test stimuli were equally spaced on a log scale, with the geometric mean of the

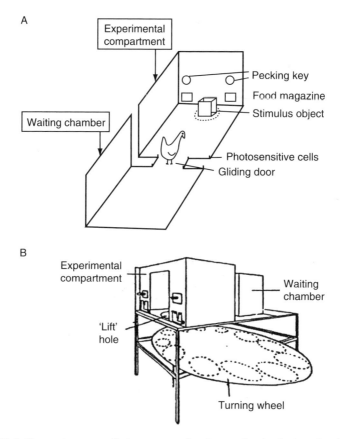

A

Experimental
compartment

Pecking key

Food magazine

Stimulus object

Waiting chamber

Photosensitive cells

Gliding door

B

Experimental
compartment

Waiting
chamber

'Lift'
hole

Turning wheel

Figure A1.1 Computer-controlled apparatus for the psychophysical study of chickens (schematic drawing): A inside view; B outside view. (Adapted from Sarris, 1990.)

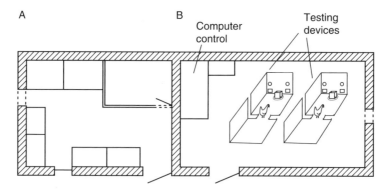

A

B

Computer
control

Testing
devices

Figure A1.2 Animal psychophysics lab (schematic *top view*): A housing and scratching field; B two computer-controlled training and testing devices, working in parallel (see Figure A1.1).

Table A1.1 Set of training and test stimuli used (general design logic)

Physical scale–volume (in ccm)	45	64	90.5	128	181	256	362	512	724	1024	1448	2048	2896
Training stimuli					215			608					
Null test series (C0)				128	181	256	**362**	512	724	1024			
Small contextual test series (C1)	45	64	90.5	128	181	256	**362**						
Large contextual test series (C2)							**362**	512	724	1024	1448	2048	2896

Note. Subjects were trained with two successively presented training stimuli (TS) and tested with different test series either symmetrically (C0) or asymmetrically distributed to the TS (C1, C2). The stimulus value **362** is middle-sized under C0, the largest under C1, and the smallest under C2.

two training stimuli defining the midpoint of the null test series (C0). For the small contextual series, C1, the geometric mean of the training stimuli was the largest of the test stimuli; for the large contextual series, C2, this was the smallest of the test stimuli.

Procedure

Typically, the experiment included three phases for each subject: (a) key training; (b) discrimination training; (c) generalization testing. After key training the subjects were trained to peck key 1 if TS 1, i.e. the 215 ccm cube was presented, however to peck key 2 if TS 2, i.e., the 608 cube was provided. The daily training sessions consisted of 50 trials each. The stimulus sequence was randomly determined each day with the restriction that each stimulus was presented with equal frequency.

At the start of each trial the subject was held in the illuminated waiting box while a cube was positioned in the test box. Then the light was turned off in the waiting box while the light in the test box was turned on and the gliding door was opened. Following this brightness shift, the subject entered the test box. If it pecked the correct key this key choice was reinforced by access to the food magazine for three seconds. Then the test box was darkened, the waiting box was illuminated again, and so forth. Darkness immediately followed an incorrect key choice and the same stimulus was presented again after six seconds.

After reaching the learning criterion, usually 95 per cent correct choices for three successive training sessions, the six subjects were assigned randomly to the three post-generalization test conditions (C0, C1, C2). Each test series was presented six times daily during six successive test days. *All choices were reinforced during the test stage*.

Note

The apparatus used for the *infant chicks* is described in the main text (see chapter 4, Figure 4.6; for more details see Sarris, 1998).

Appendix 2

Mathematics of transposition and psychophysics

The general mathematics of *transposition*, as developed here in view of a psychophysics of stimulus relations, is described in chapter 3 of this monograph (see also chapter 5). Its mathematical refinement is presented as follows (Gregson & Sarris, 1985, unpubl.; see also Gregson, 1988, 1992):

Remember that the transposition problem is known as a demonstration that human and animal subjects will *shift* their perceptual judgements if the *ranges* of stimuli presented are displaced from an original range that is bounded within the limits that the organism can usually accept. In this paradigm we have two training stimuli (T_1 and T_2), and a stimulus series {S} which extends noticeably both above and below the range $D_T = \text{abs}(T_1 - T_2)$ so that $T_2 > T_1$; $T_1, T_2, \in$ {S}. The subject, from any stimulus X, X $\in$ {S}, is asked to make an allocation decision of it to one of two responses <1> or <2>, such as:

$$X \rightarrow <1> \quad \text{or} \quad X \rightarrow <2> \tag{E1}$$

and the relation between observed <i> i= 1,2 whereby D_T:X (where D_T:X means the training range used for stimulus X) with the composition of {S}. This behaviour is interpreted as a *PSI shift* associated with {S} so that irrespective of (D_T, T_1), the PSI value drifts monotonically in time to somewhere in the middle of the range of {S}. This behaviour is consistent with the *FR* notion concerning the *sequential shifting* of the PSI (see chapter 3, e.g. Figure 3.1).

The basis of this allocation decision can be either a judgement of *relative similarity*, such as R (X; T_1, T_2), or a judgment of relative differences D (X; T_1, T_2). It is easy to show with set theoretic *similarity* measures that a paradox results if we use R, so that all points X' > T_2 or X' < T_1, have equal R and this is solely a function of (T_1, T_2). This result may seem counter-intuitive, but it implies that if we constructed a D, R task (*similarity* judgement) from {R}, {S}, T_1, T_2, then the observed behaviour would be different from that induced by a decision task as suggested in (E1). We now look at what happens if (E1) is based on judgements of *absolute differences* of stimulus magnitudes. As the stimuli are deliberately unidimensional, and only vary, say, in size or in colour, it is without loss of generality admissible to treat the *ratio* of the differences (RD) as lying in a one-dimensional city-block space, and then to define:

$$RD\,(X;\,T_1,\,T_2) = \frac{\text{Abs}\,(X - T_1)}{\text{Abs}\,(X - T_2)}, \text{ where } T_2 > X > T_1 \qquad (E2)$$

Consider now a point $X' > T_2$ (the argument for $X' < T_1$ is analogous and hence omitted here). It is possible for some X to find an X' corresponding to X, in the sense that:

$$RD\,(X';\,T_1,\,T_2) = RD\,(X;\,T_1,\,T_2), \qquad (E3)$$

which means:

$$\frac{\text{Abs}\,(X' - T_1)}{\text{Abs}\,(X' - T_2)} = \frac{\text{Abs}\,(X - T_1)}{\text{Abs}\,(X - T_2)}, \text{ given } X,\,T_1,\,T_2 \qquad (E4)$$

This implies that there exists a continuous range of X' values for the X values, given some T_1, T_2, which also satisfy the *ratio* of relative distances RD. This is algebraically trivial, but the interest lies in what happens if RD is the basis of a *decision rule*. We write the rule without stochastic noise, as the variation in the internal representation of the members of the series {X} is sufficient to induce such noise in a more detailed formulation, namely:

If $X \in \{S\}$ and $X' \in \{S\}$ then only

$(X;\,T_1,\,T_2)$ can serve as a basis for

$X \rightarrow <1>. <2>$ as $D\,(X,\,T_1) > D\,(X,\,T_2)$ \qquad (E5)

If $X' \in \{S\}$ and $X \in \{S\}$ then only

$(X':\,T_1,\,T_2)$ can serve as a basis for

$X' \rightarrow <1>, <2>$ as $D\,(X',\,T_1) > D\,(X',\,T_2)$ \qquad (E6)

That is, if {S} spans one but not both of X, $X' \in \{S\}$ then (E5) or (E6) operate. However, if S spans both, that is X, $X' \in \{S\}$, then the behaviour for that set of $(X, X') \in \{S\}$ is ambiguous and may be determined if we can calculate RD (Y; X, X') as a basis for a rule like (E5) where X, X', $Y \in \{S\}$ and $X < Y < X'$.

Note

A full chapter about the *nonlinear* version of the mathematics for the transposition and range effects has been provided in the monograph by Robert A. M. Gregson (1988, chapter 12).

Appendix 3

An engine model of relational psychophysics

Stuart Anstis and Viktor Sarris

A simple *engine model* of the chicken's relational psychophysics is outlined below. It is based on the assumption of the organism's minimum cognitive capacities. For a more lengthy version see Anstis and Sarris (2006). As to the general procedure the reader is referred to chapter 3 (pp. 43–45; see also Appendix 2).

Training and testing

First of all, the chicken must be trained to discriminate a large cube from a small one. The bird views a wooden cube and two pecking keys; one large and one small cube are varied across trials. To keep the numbers simple, let us suppose that the side of the cube is either 2 cm or 4 cm. The chicken's task is to peck the left-hand key if the cube is "large" and the right-hand key if the cube is "small", or vice versa. Correct responses are rewarded with a small amount of food. This apparently simple task can take a chicken three weeks or more to learn even if it practises one hour every day (Sarris, e.g. 1994). When it reaches a criterion of 95 per cent correct in two successive sessions it is considered to be trained. The testing phase begins and one can investigate *context effects* during the post-discrimination generalization phase (test phase), in which the chicken is shown a series of test cubes of different sizes. (Typically the chicken is retrained between test runs to maintain its performance at the criterion level.) During testing, the chicken is shown a new series of cubes of sizes 1, **2**, 3, **4**, 5. These five test cubes are presented repeatedly in random order and the experimenter records the percentage of trials on which each cube size evokes a peck on, say, the right-hand key (small cube).

Three possible context effects: asymmetrical shifts, range effects and frequency effects

Asymmetrical shifts

The test series of 1, **2**, 3, **4**, 5 can be displaced upwards by adding a constant number of cm to each size, such as 3 (new testing range = **4**, 5, 6, 7, 8) or shifted downwards by 0.5 (new testing range = 0.5, 1.5, 2.5, 3.5, 4.5).

Compressed and expanded ranges

A compressed range can be used, still with a mean size of 3, but with a step size of 0.5 instead of 1 cm, thus: **2**, 2.5, 3, 3.5, **4**. An expanded range might have a step size of, say, 1.25; thus: 0.5, 1.75, 3, 4.25, 5.5.

Frequency distributions

For a rectangular distribution, the sizes 1, **2**, 3, **4**, 5 cm are presented equally often. For a triangular distribution favouring large sizes, the range of sizes remains at 1, **2**, 3, **4**, 5 but the frequency distribution is altered, such that the smallest size of 1 cm is presented only once, the 2 cm cube is presented twice, the 3 cm cube 3 times, the 4 cm cube 4 times and the 5 cm cube 5 times. In other words, the following set of sizes is presented in random order: 1, **2**, **2**, 3, 3, 3, **4**, **4**, **4**, **4**, 5, 5, 5, 5, 5 cm. For a triangular distribution favouring small sizes, the range of sizes remains at 1, **2**, 3, **4**, 5 but now the smallest size of 1 cm is presented 5 times, the 2 cm cube is presented 4 times, the 3 cm cube 3 times, the 4 cm cube twice and the 5 cm cube only once. In other words, the following set of sizes is presented in random order: 1, 1, 1, 1, 1, **2**, **2**, **2**, **2**, 3, 3, 3, **4**, **4**, 5 *cm*.

The engine model

Note that the model ("engine model") is presented in the form of an "imaginary chicken", that knows nothing about running averages, ranges, frequencies, nor about excitatory or inhibitory processes. Instead, it uses a very simple strategy that allows it to generate the experimental results, while knowing nothing about the statistics of the stimuli. The aim of the engine model as described below is to *mimic* as much of the behaviour of a real chicken as possible, in order to define as parsimoniously as feasible a lower bound on the abilities of real chickens (*Occam's razor*).

The logic of the engine model

Now imagine a hypothetical situation in which at the end of each trial the experimenter puts the old cube on a shelf and leaves it there, in full view of the imaginary chicken, while the next (new) cube is presented. As for human psychophysics models it is suggested that in this comparative task the chicken will not examine the absolute size of the new cube, but will respond only by pecking the large key if the new cube is larger than the still visible old cube, and by pecking the small key if the new cube is smaller than the old cube. In other words, the chicken is a *difference engine*, responding only to the successive difference in the stimuli, namely the difference in size between successive cubes. Of course there is no actual "shelf" in the experiment on which to store the old cube. The proposal here is that the shelf is in the chicken's *memory* and that in every case the chicken is responding simply to the difference in size between the present stimulus and the remembered previous stimulus. It may be claimed that this simple strategy will generate most or all of the context effects with which the respective literature – at least, with lower animals – is filled. Imagine a series of random permutations of 1, 2, 3, 4, 5 cm; part of such a randomized permutation series might run as shown below:

Number:	4	2	1	5	3	3	2	5	1	4
Difference:		–	–	+	–	=	–	+	–	+

Below each number is a sign (+, –, or =), that shows whether that number is larger (+) or smaller (–) than the number to its left. Thus, under the second digit (2) is a minus sign because 2 is smaller than 4. The third digit (1) also has a minus sign under it because 1 is smaller than 2. The 5 has a plus sign because 5 is greater than 1, and so on. In this model, the row of *plus* and *minus* signs predicts the chicken's responses: Note again that the model chicken responds only to the *sign* (positive or negative) of the difference between successive cubes, and is blind to the absolute magnitude of these differences. It is also blind to the absolute values of the numbers themselves, responding for instance with a *minus* (–) to the first 3 that it sees (because 3 is less than the 5 that it follows) but with a *plus* (+) to the second 3 (because 3 is larger than the 2 that it follows).

One could do a *Monte Carlo* simulation of such an experiment by generating a long string of such digits between 1 and 5, noting the difference (–, +, =) which the model predicts for the chicken's response, and tabulating the results. But one may save the trouble by tabulating simply all possible digits 1 through 5 and their *immediate* predecessors in time, as shown in Table A3.1.

Predicted context effects

We now look at the context effects.

Asymmetrical shift

Suppose that a novel set of test cubes is presented, of sides 4, 5, 6, 7 and 8 cm. The predicted results are shown in Table A3.2.

Table A3.1 Range 1, 2, 3, 4, 5

Size of previous stimulus (cm) →

Size of present stimulus V	1	2	3	4	5	Number of larger (+) responses	% of + responses (normalized)
1	=	–	–	–	–	0 / 4	0
2	+	=	–	–	–	1 / 4	25
3	+	+	=	–	–	2 / 4	50
4	+	+	+	=	–	3 / 4	75
5	+	+	+	+	=	4 / 4	100
Total + responses						10 / 20	

Table A3.2 Asymmetrical shift 4, 5, 6, 7, 8

Size of previous stimulus (cm) →

Size of present stimulus V	4	5	6	7	8	Number of larger (+) responses	% of + responses (normalized)
4	=	–	–	–	–	0 / 4	0
5	+	=	–	–	–	1 / 4	25
6	+	+	=	–	–	2 / 4	50
7	+	+	+	=	–	3 / 4	75
8	+	+	+	+	=	4 / 4	100
Total + responses						10 / 20	

The hypothetical chicken will *transfer* ("transpose") exactly the responses it made when the range was 1, **2**, 3, **4**, 5 to the new range of 4, 5, 6, 7, 8. In fact, Table A3.2 is identical to Table A3.1 except that the number 3 has been added to every stimulus size. Thus the model predicts a perfect transposition of the chicken's responses, such that a graphic plot of the responses will simply be slid horizontally to the right.

Compressed range

Suppose that the previous test range of 1, 2, 3, 4, 5 is still centred on a mean value of 3 but is now compressed, with the step size reduced from 1 cm to 0.5 cm, resulting in a compressed range of 2, 2.5, 3, 3.5, 4. The results for the model are shown in Table A3.3.

The responses are now compressed to match exactly the new compressed set of test stimuli. In fact, Table A3.3 is exactly the same as Table A3.1 except

Table A3.3 Compressed range 2, 2.5, 3, 3.5, 4

Size of previous stimulus (cm) →

Size of present stimulus V	2	2.5	3	3.5	4	Number of larger (+) responses	% of + responses (normalized)
2	=	−	−	−	−	0 / 4	0
2.5	+	=	−	−	−	1 / 4	25
3	+	+	=	−	−	2 / 4	50
3.5	+	+	+	=	−	3 / 4	75
4	+	+	+	+	=	4 / 4	100
Total + responses						10 / 20	

that the stimulus values have been altered from 1, 2, 3, 4, 5 to 2, 2.5, 3, 3.5, 4. When plotted as a function of absolute stimulus size, the chicken's responses are *compressed*. There is nothing magical about this, because our bird has no interest at all in absolute size but is responding only to the *differences* in size – and not even to differences measured in cm but only to rank order. Furthermore, our imaginary chicken never even arranges a set of five stimuli such as 1, 2, 3, 4, 5 or 2, 2.5, 3, 3.5, 4 into rank order, but makes only pairwise comparisons.

Frequency distributions

Table A3.3 tabulates all possible results for a *rectangular* distribution of cube sizes 1, 2, 3, 4 and 5 cm, in which all sizes were equally probable. Now consider frequency distributions that also use stimulus sizes of 1, 2, 3, 4, 5 in favour of some sizes over others by presenting them more or less frequently. Table A3.4(a) and Table A3.4(b) show two *triangular* distributions, in which the different cube sizes are unequally represented. The distribution in Table A3.4(b) favours large cubes, so it comprises one cube of size 1 cm, two cubes of size 2 cm, three cubes of size 3 cm, four cubes of size 4 cm and five cubes of size 5 cm; on the other hand, the distribution in Table A3.4(a) favours small cubes, so it comprises five cubes of size 1 cm, four cubes of size 2 cm, three cubes of size 3 cm, two cubes of size 4 cm and one cube of size 5 cm.

Tables A3.5 and A3.6 show the hypothetical responses that the imaginary chicken makes to these distributions. The columns show the size of the cube that immediately precedes each judgement, and the rows show the size of each cube presently being judged. A plus sign (or a minus sign) in a cell indicates that the present cube is judged as larger (or smaller) than its predecessor. Assume again that the imaginary chicken is a perfect judge of *plus* and *minus*. An equals sign in a cell indicates that the same sized cube is shown twice in succession. These equals cells are omitted from all calculations (in the

Table A3.4 Two triangular distributions of cube sizes:

(a) distribution favours small cubes (see Table A3.5);

(b) distribution favours large cubes (see Table A3.6).

a						b					
	1	2	3	4	5		1	2	3	4	5
	1	2	3	4				2	3	4	5
	1	2	3						3	4	5
	1	2								4	5
	1										5

model they would provoke a "larger" or "smaller" response on a 50/50 random basis).

Tables A3.5 and A3.6 are symmetrical, with the major equal cells running along the negative diagonal and with equal numbers of plus and minus cells lying respectively below and above this diagonal. There are a total of $15 \times 15 = 225$ cells in each table, but $(1^2 + 2^2 + 3^2 + 4^2 + 5^2) = 55$ cells are the respective "equal" cells. Since, by symmetry, there are equal numbers of plus cells and minus cells (85 of each out of a total of 170 white cells), this model predicts a perfectly performing chicken will respond with "greater than" on 50 per cent of the trials for both distributions. However, this 50 per cent will be differently arranged in the two distributions. For instance, when there are more large cubes, as in Table A3.5, each 2 cm cube will elicit a "greater than" response only once, because there is only one cube smaller than 2 cm (namely, the single 1 cm cube). Since there are only two 2 cm cubes in the distribution, the 2 cm cubes will contribute a total of only two out of the total 85 "larger" responses. On the other hand, when there are more small cubes, as in Table A3.6, each 2 cm cube will elicit five "greater than" responses, because there are five cubes smaller than 2 cm (namely, the five 1cm cubes). Since there are four 2 cm cubes in the distribution, the 2 cm cubes will contribute a total of 20 out of the total 85 "larger" responses. Thus, the 2 cm cubes contributed a total of ten times as many + responses in Table A3.6 than in Table A3.5.

Predictions: effects of relative frequency of cube sizes

Figure A3.1 plots the hypothetical pecks made by an imaginary chicken to a cube drawn from a randomly ordered triangular distribution favouring cubes of small sizes (*upper curve*, open symbols) and large sizes (*lower curve*, filled symbols). These hypothetical responses are taken from Tables A3.5 and A3.6, second column from the right. For instance, in the upper curve (many small cubes) there are five 1 cm cubes, so a 2 cm cube (x = 2) has five changes of following a 1 cm cube and eliciting a + response (y = 5). In the lower curve (many large cubes) there is only one 1 cm cube so a 2 cm cube (x = 2) has only one chance of following it and eliciting a + response (y = 1). Each cube in the

Table A3.5 Distribution favouring large numbers

Prev→ now V	1	2	2	3	3	3	4	4	4	4	5	5	5	5	5	# −	# +	Max
1	=	−	−	−	−	−	−	−	−	−	−	−	−	−	−	14	0	14
2	+	=	=	−	−	−	−	−	−	−	−	−	−	−	−	12	1	13
2	+	=	=	−	−	−	−	−	−	−	−	−	−	−	−	12	1	13
3	+	+	+	=	=	=	−	−	−	−	−	−	−	−	−	9	3	12
3	+	+	+	=	=	=	−	−	−	−	−	−	−	−	−	9	3	12
3	+	+	+	=	=	=	−	−	−	−	−	−	−	−	−	9	3	12
4	+	+	+	+	+	+	=	=	=	=	−	−	−	−	−	5	6	11
4	+	+	+	+	+	+	=	=	=	=	−	−	−	−	−	5	6	11
4	+	+	+	+	+	+	=	=	=	=	−	−	−	−	−	5	6	11
4	+	+	+	+	+	+	=	=	=	=	−	−	−	−	−	5	6	11
5	+	+	+	+	+	+	+	+	+	+	=	=	=	=	=	0	10	10
5	+	+	+	+	+	+	+	+	+	+	=	=	=	=	=	0	10	10
5	+	+	+	+	+	+	+	+	+	+	=	=	=	=	=	0	10	10
5	+	+	+	+	+	+	+	+	+	+	=	=	=	=	=	0	10	10
5	+	+	+	+	+	+	+	+	+	+	=	=	=	=	=	0	10	10
Total																85	85	170

Table A3.6 Distribution favouring small numbers

Prev→	1	1	1	1	1	2	2	2	2	3	3	3	4	4	5	#−	#+	Max
now V																		
1	=	=	=	=	=	−	−	−	−	−	−	−	−	−	−	10	0	10
1	=	=	=	=	=	−	−	−	−	−	−	−	−	−	−	10	0	10
1	=	=	=	=	=	−	−	−	−	−	−	−	−	−	−	10	0	10
1	=	=	=	=	=	−	−	−	−	−	−	−	−	−	−	10	0	10
1	=	=	=	=	=	−	−	−	−	−	−	−	−	−	−	10	0	10
2	+	+	+	+	+	=	=	=	=	−	−	−	−	−	−	6	5	11
2	+	+	+	+	+	=	=	=	=	−	−	−	−	−	−	6	5	11
2	+	+	+	+	+	=	=	=	=	−	−	−	−	−	−	6	5	11
2	+	+	+	+	+	=	=	=	=	−	−	−	−	−	−	6	5	11
3	+	+	+	+	+	+	+	+	+	=	=	=	−	−	−	3	9	12
3	+	+	+	+	+	+	+	+	+	=	=	=	−	−	−	3	9	12
3	+	+	+	+	+	+	+	+	+	=	=	=	−	−	−	3	9	12
4	+	+	+	+	+	+	+	+	+	+	+	+	=	=	−	1	12	13
4	+	+	+	+	+	+	+	+	+	+	+	+	=	=	−	1	12	13
5	+	+	+	+	+	+	+	+	+	+	+	+	+	+	=	0	14	14
Total																85	85	170

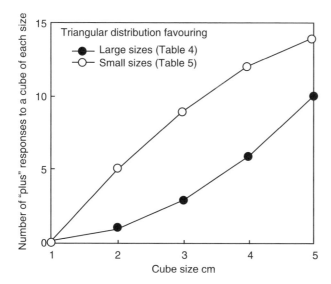

Figure A3.1 Hypothetical pecks made by an imaginary chicken to different sized cubes under two test-series conditions (C1, C2): *upper curve*: test series containing many small cubes; *lower curve*; test series containing many large cubes.

lower curve elicits fewer + responses than in the upper curve, but to compensate for this there are more large cubes in the distribution so that the total + responses in each case add up to 85 (= 50 per cent of all trials). Thus, it is predicted that a chicken's responses to cubes of each size will be strongly influenced by the relative frequency of these sizes in the stimulus distribution. It should be added that this very parsimonious engine model of relational psychophysics allows further predictions, for instance, those of order effects (ascending versus descending event frequencies; see Anstis & Sarris, 2006).

Note

For a general account of the *neuro-informatics* of a behaving organism see, for instance, Bateson and Horn, 1994; Bolhuis, 1999; Braitenberg (1984); Churchland and Sejnowski, 1992/1999; Enquist and Ghirlanda (2005); Erlhagen (2003); Erlhagen and Jahnke (2004); see also Erlhagen and Schöner (2002); Ghirlanda (2002, 2005); Ghirlanda and Enquist (2003); O'Reilly and Johnson, 1994; Solan and Ruppin, 2001; Tarr and Bülthoff (1998).

References

Actis-Grosso, R., & Vezziani, S. (2003). Rediscoveries in perception: Toward a database. In B. Berglund & E. Borg (Eds.), *Fechner Day 2003: Proceedings of the 19th Annual Meeting of the International Society for Psychophysics* (pp. 1–6). Larnaca/Cyprus: ISP.

Ahissar, M., & Hochstein, S. (2004). The reverse hierarchy theory of visual learning. *Trends in Cognitive Sciences, 8*, 340–348.

Albright, T. D., Croner, L. J., Duncan, R. O., & Stoner, G. R. (2003). Neuronal correlates of perceptual organization in the primate visual system. In R. Kimchi, M. Behrmann, & C. R. Olson (Eds.), *Perceptual organization in vision: Behavioral and neural perspectives* (pp. 305–335). Mahwah, NJ: Lawrence Erlbaum Associates, Inc.

Algom, D. (Ed.). (1992). *Psychophysical approaches to cognition.* Amsterdam: North-Holland.

Algom, D. (2003). Psychophysics. In L. Nadel (Ed.), *Encyclopaedia of cognitive science.* (Vol. 3, pp. 800–805). New York: Nature.

Allman, J. M. (1999). *Evolving brains.* New York: Scientific American Library.

Allman, J., Miezin, F., & McGuiness, E. (1985). Stimulus-specific responses from beyond the classical receptive field: Neurophysiological mechanisms for local-global comparisons in visual neurons. *Review of Neuroscience, 8*, 407–430.

Anderson, N. H. (1975). On the role of context effects in psychophysical judgements. *Psychological Review, 82*, 462–482.

Anderson, N. H. (1983). Cognitive algebra in intuitive physics. In H.-G. Geissler, H. F. J. M. Buffart, E. L. J. Leeuwenberg, & V. Sarris (Eds.), *Modern issues in perception* (pp. 229–253). Amsterdam: North-Holland.

Anderson, N. H. (2001). *Empirical direction in design and analysis.* Mahwah, NJ: Lawrence Erlbaum Associates, Inc.

Andrew, R. J. (Ed.). (1991). *Neural and behavioural plasticity: The use of the domestic chick as a model.* Oxford: Oxford University Press.

Angermeier, W. F. (1984). *The evolution of operant learning and memory: Comparative etho-psychology.* Basel: Karger Press.

Anstis, S., & Sarris, V. (2006). *Context effects in animal psychophysics: Smart strategies from simple-minded chickens?* (In preparation.)

Ash, M. G. (1995). *Gestalt psychology in German culture 1890–1967: Holism and the quest for objectivity.* Cambridge, MA: Cambridge University Press.

Aslin, R. N., & Fiser, J. (2005). Methodological challenges for understanding cognitive development in infants. *Trends in Cognitive Sciences, 9*, 92–98.

Atkinson, J. (2000). *The developing visual brain*. Oxford: Oxford University Press.

Atkinson, J., & Braddick, O. (1999). Research methods in infant vision. In R. H. S. Carpenter & J. G. Robson (Eds.), *Vision research: A practical guide to laboratory methods* (pp. 161–186). Oxford: Oxford University Press.

Avant, L. L. (1965). Vision in the Ganzfeld. *Psychological Bulletin, 64*, 246–258.

Bahrick, L. E. (1992). Infants' perceptual differentiation of amodal and modality-specific audio-visual relations. *Journal of Experimental Child Psychology, 53*, 197–209.

Bahrick, L. E. (2000). Increasing specifity in the development of intermodal perception. In D. Muir & A. Slater (Eds.), *Infant development: The essential readings* (pp. 119–136). Hillsdale, NJ: Lawrence Erlbaum Associates, Inc.

Baillargeon, R. (1993). The object concept revisited: New directions in the investigation of infants' physical knowledge. In C. Granrud (Ed.), *Visual perception and cognition in infancy* (pp. 265–315). Hillsdale, NJ: Lawrence Erlbaum Associates, Inc.

Baird, J. C. (1970). Three philosophies of measurement. In J. C. Baird, *Psychophysical analysis of visual space* (pp. 300–310). Oxford: Pergamon.

Baird, J. C. (1997). *Sensation and judgment: Complementarity theory of psychophysics*. Mahwah, NJ: Lawrence Erlbaum Associates, Inc.

Balsam, P. D., & Tomie, A. (Eds.). (1985). *Context and learning*. Hillsdale, NJ: Lawrence Erlbaum Associates, Inc.

Bateson, P. P. G. (1991). Making sense of behavioural development in the chick. In R. J. Andrew (Ed.), *Neural and behavioural plasticity: The use of the domestic chick as a model* (pp. 113–132). Oxford: Oxford University Press.

Bateson, P., & Horn, G. (1994). Imprinting and recognition memory: A neural net model. *Animal Behaviour, 48*, 695–715.

Bekoff, M., Allen, C., & Burkhardt, G. M. (Eds.). (2002). *The cognitive animal: Empirical and theoretical perspectives in animal cognition*. Cambridge, MA: MIT Press.

Beniuc, M. (1932). Bedeutungswechsel der Dinge in der Umwelt des Kampffisches *Betta splendens Regan*. [Change of meaning of environmental objects in the fighting fish *Betta splendens Regan*.] *Zeitschrift für Vergleichende Physiologie, 18*, 437–458.

Beniuc, M. (1933). Bewegungssehen, Verschmelzung und Moment bei Kampffischen. [Visual motion, flicker frequency and the moment of the fighting fish.] *Zeitschrift für Vergleichende Physiologie, 19*, 724–746.

Beran, M. J. (2004). Chimpanzees (*pan troglodytes*) respond to nonvisible sets after one-by-one addition and removal of items. *Journal of Comparative Psychology, 118*, 25–36.

Beran, M. J., & Beran, M. M. (2004). Chimpanzees remember the results of one-by-one addition of food items to sets over extended time periods. *Psychological Science, 15*, 94–95.

Berglund, B., & Borg, E. (Eds.). (2003). *Fechner Day 2003: Proceedings of the 19th Annual Meeting of the International Society for Psychophysics*. Stockholm: ISP.

Berkley, M. A., & Stebbins, W. C. (Eds.). (1990). *Comparative perception (Vol. 1): Basic mechanisms*. New York: Wiley.

Birnbaum, M. H. (1974). Using contextual effects to derive psychophysical scales. *Perception and Psychophysics, 15*, 89–96.

Bitterman, M. E. (2000). Cognitive evolution: A psychological perspective. In C. Heyes & L. Huber (Eds.), *Evolution of cognition* (pp. 61–79). Cambridge, MA: MIT Press.

Blake, R. (1999). The behavioral analysis of animal vision. In R. H. S. Carpenter &

J. G. Robson (Eds.), *Vision research: A practical guide to laboratory methods* (pp. 137–160). Oxford: Oxford University Press.

Blough, D. S. (2001). *The perception of similarity*. Retrieved January 2004, from http://www.pigeon.psy.tufts.edu/avc/toc.htm

Bolhuis, J. J. (1999). The development of animal behaviour: From Lorenz to neural nets. *Naturwissenschaften, 86*, 101–111.

Boring, E. G. (1942). *Sensation and perception in the history of experimental psychology*. New York: Appleton-Century-Crofts.

Bornstein, M. H. (1999). Human infancy: Past, present, future. In M. Bennet (Ed.), *Developmental psychology: Achievements and Prospects* (pp. 13–35). Hove, UK: Psychology Press.

Bower, T. G. R. (1966). The visual world of infants. *Scientific American, 215*, 80–92.

Bower, T. G. R. (1977). *The perceptual world of the child*. London: Fontana.

Brainerd, C. J. (1981). Working memory and developmental analysis of probability judgment. *Psychological Review, 88*, 463–502.

Brainerd, C. J. (Ed.). (1983). *Recent advances in cognitive-developmental theory*. New York: Wiley.

Brainerd, C. J., & Reyna, V. F. (1990). Inclusion illusions: Fuzzy trace theory and perceptual salience effects in cognitive development. *Developmental Review, 10*, 365–403.

Brainerd, C. J., & Reyna, V. F. (1993). Memory independence and memory interference in cognitive development. *Psychological Review, 100*, 42–67.

Brainerd, C. J., & Reyna, V. F. (1994). Domains of fuzzy trace theory. In M. L. Howe & R. Pasnak (Eds.), *Emerging themes in cognitive-developmental theory* (pp. 74–89). New York: Springer Verlag.

Braitenberg, V. (1984). *Vehicles: Experiments in synthetic psychology*. Cambridge, MA: MIT Press.

Brecher, G. A. (1933). Die Entstehung und biologische Bedeutung der subjektiven Zeiteinheit – des Momentes. [The origin and biological significance of the subjective temporal unit – the moment.] *Zeitschrift für Vergleichende Physiologie, 18*, 204–243.

Bredenkamp, J., & Sarris, V. (1987). Psychophysics today: Contemporary research in the Fed. Rep. of Germany. *German Journal of Psychology, 11*, 179–197.

Bremner, J. G. (2001). Cognitive development: Knowledge of the physical world. In J. G. Bremner & A. Fogel (Eds.), *Blackwell handbook of infant development* (pp. 99–138). Oxford: Blackwell.

Bremner, J. G., & Fogel, A. (Eds.). (2001). *Blackwell handbook of infant development*. Oxford: Blackwell.

Brown, D. R. (1953). Stimulus-similarity and the anchoring of subjective scales. *American Journal of Psychology, 66*, 199–214.

Bruce, V., Green, P. R., & Georgeson, M. A. (1996). *Visual perception* (3rd ed.). Hove, UK: Psychology Press.

Bryant, P. (1974). *Perception and understanding in young children*. London: Methuen.

Bülthoff, I., Bülthoff, H. H., & Sinha, P. (1998). Top-down influences on stereoscopic depth-perception. *Nature Neuroscience, 1*, 254–257.

Bunge, M. (1983). *Exploring the world*. Dordrecht: Reidel.

Bunge, M., & Ardila, R. (1987). *Philosophy of psychology*. New York: Springer.

Cangöz, B. N. (1999). *Wahrnehmungs- und Urteilsrelativität bei Erwachsenen und Kindern: Psychophysikalische Bezugssystemeffekte in der Zeitwahrnehmung.*

[Perceptual-judgemental relativity in adults and children: Psychophysical frame-of-reference effects in time perception.] Frankfurt a.M.: Lang.

Cantor, J. H., & Spiker, C. C. (1989). Children's learning revisited: The contemporary scope of the modified Spence discrimination theory. *Advances in Child Development and Behavior*, *21*, 121–151.

Casco, C., Grieco, A., & Giora, E. (2003). The relation between saliency of motion and form. In B. Berglund & E. Borg (Eds.), *Fechner Day 2003: Proceedings of the 16th Annual Meeting of the International Society for Psychophysics* (pp. 43–46). Stockholm: ISP.

Cataliotti, J., & Gilchrist, A. (1995). Local and global processes in surface lightness perception. *Perception and Psychophysics*, *57*, 125–135.

Chalupa, L. M., & Werner, J. S. (Eds.). (2004). *The visual neurosciences* (2 Vols.). Cambridge, MA: MIT Press.

Chase, S. (1983). Pigeons and the magical number seven. In M. L. Commons, R. J. Herrnstein, & A. R. Wagner (Eds.), *Quantitative analyses of behavior: Discrimination processes* (Vol. 4, pp. 37–57). Cambridge, MA: Ballinger.

Chase, S. (1997). "Concept formation" and categorization by pigeons. In S. Watanabe & S. Chase (Eds.), *Pattern recognition in humans and animals* (pp. 11–17). Tokyo: Keio University Press.

Chase, S., & Heinemann, E. (2001). *Exemplar memory and discrimination*. Retrieved January 2004, from http://www.pigeon.psy.tufts.edu/avc/toc.htm

Chien, S. H. L., Palmer, J., & Teller, D. Y. (2003). Infant lightness perception: Do 4-month-old infants follow Wallach's ratio? *Psychological Science*, *14*, 291–295.

Chun, M. M. (2005). Drug-induced amnesia impairs implicit relational memory. *Trends in Cognitive Sciences*, *9*, 355–357.

Church, R. M. (2003). Time perception. In L. Nadel (Ed.), *Encyclopedia of cognitive science* (Vol. 4, pp. 398–400). New York: Nature.

Churchland, P. S., & Sejnowski, T. J. (Eds.). (1992/1999). *The computational brain*. Cambridge, MA: MIT Press.

Cook, R. G. (Ed.). (2001). *Avian visual cognition*. Retrieved January 2004 from http://www.pigeon.psy.tufts.edu/avc/toc.htm

Corballis, M. (2003). Evolution of the human brain. In L. Nadel (Ed.), *Encyclopedia of cognitive science* (Vol. 2, pp. 386–392). New York: Nature.

Coren, S., & Enns, J. T. (1993). Size contrast as a function of conceptual similarity between test and inducers. *Perception and Psychophysics*, *34*, 539–554.

Coren, S., & Miller, J. (1974). Size contrast as a function of figural similarity. *Perception and Psychophysics*, *16*, 355–357.

Costall, A., Sinico, M., & Parovel, G. (2003). The concept of invariants and the problem of perceptual constancy. *Rivista di estetica*, *24*, 45–49.

Cowey, A., & Walsh, V. (2001). Tickling the brain: Studying visual sensation, perception and cognition by transcranial magnetic stimulation. *Progress in Brain Research*, *134*, 411–425.

Cruz, J. (2003). Epistemology. In L. Nadel (Ed.), *Encyclopedia of cognitive science* (Vol. 1, pp. 23–28). New York: Nature.

Cynx, J. (1995). Similarities in absolute and relative pitch perception in songbirds (starling and zebra finch) and nonsongbird (pigeon). *Journal of Comparative Psychology*, *109*, 261–267.

Dassler, K. (2000). *Altersspezifische Kontexteffekte bei der Wahrnehmung und*

Beurteilung von Reizgrößen. [Age-specific context effects in the perception and judgement of stimulus-sizes.] Unpublished doctoral dissertation: Frankfurt University.

Dassler, K., & Sarris, V. (1997, July). *Context effects in psychophysics: Size judgments with different age groups.* Paper presented at the Vth European Congress of Psychology, Dublin, Ireland. (Cited after Sarris, 2004.)

DeCarlo, L. T. (1994). A dynamic theory of proportional judgment: Context and judgment of length, heaviness, and roughness. *Journal of Experimental Psychology: Human Perception and Performance, 20,* 372–381.

DeCarlo, L. T. (2003). An application of a dynamic model of judgment to magnitude production. *Perception and Psychophysics, 65,* 152–162.

DeCarlo, L. T., & Cross, D. V. (1990). Sequential effects in magnitude scaling: Models and theory. *Journal of Experimental Psychology: General, 119,* 275–396.

Dehaene, S. (1997). *The number sense.* New York: Oxford University Press.

Dehaene, S. (2003). The neural basis of the Weber-Fechner law: A logarithmic mental number line. *Trends in Cognitive Sciences, 7,* 145–147.

De Lillo, C., Floreano, D., & Antinucci, F. (2001). Transitive choices by a simple, fully connected, backpropagation neural network: Implications for the comparative study of transitive inference. *Animal Cognition, 4,* 61–68.

Delius, J. D., Siemann, M., Emmerton, J., & Xia, L. (2001). Cognition of birds as products of evolved brains. In G. Roth & M. F. Wullimann (Eds.), *Brain evolution and cognition* (pp. 451–490). New York & Heideberg: Wiley/Spektrum.

De Loache, J. S. (2004). Scale errors by very young children: A dissociation between action planning and control. *Behavioral and Brain Sciences, 27,* 127–128.

De Weerd, P., & Pessoa, L. (2003). Introduction: Filling-in: More than meets the eye. In L. Pessoa & P. De Weerd (Eds.), *Filling-in: From perceptual completion to cortical reorganization* (pp. 1–12). Oxford: Oxford University Press.

Dewsbury, D. A. (1989). Comparative psychology, ethology, and animal behavior. *Annual Review of Psychology, 40,* 581–602.

Dewsbury, D. A. (1992). Comparative psychology and ethology: A reassessment. *American Psychologist, 47,* 208–215.

DiLollo, V., Enns, J. T., & Rensink, R. A. (2002). Short visual events: The psychophysics of re-entrant visual processes. *Journal of Experimental Psychology: General, 129,* 481–507.

Dittrich, W. H., & Lea, S. E. G. (2001). *Motion discrimination and recognition.* Retrieved January 2004, from http://www.pigeon.psy.tufts.edu.avc/dittrich/default.htm

Donis, F. J., Heinemann, E., & Chase, S. (1994). Context effects in visual pattern recognition by pigeons. *Perception and Psychophysics, 55,* 676–688.

Dresp, B. (1997). On illusory contours and their functional significance. *European Bulletin of Cognitive Psychology, 16,* 489–518.

Ehrenstein, W. H., Spillmann, L., & Sarris, V. (2003). Gestalt issues in modern neuroscience. *Axiomathes, 13,* 433–458.

Ehrenstein, W. H., Hamada, J., & Paramei, G. V. (2004). Size induction: Stimulus and brain correlates. In A. M. Oliveira, M. Teixeira, G. F. Borges, & M. J. Ferro (Eds.), *Fechner Day 2004: Proceedings of the 20th Annual Meeting of the International Society for Psychophysics* (pp. 70–75). Coimbra, Portugal: ISP.

Elfering, A. (1997). *Psychophysikalische Methoden und Ergebnisse in der Bezugssystemforschung: Die Rolle des Gedächtnisses im Reizgeneralisationsversuch.* [Psychophysical methods and findings from frame-of-reference research: The role of memory in the stimulus-discrimination paradigm.] Unpublished doctoral dissertation: Frankfurt University.

Elfering, A., & Sarris, V. (2005). Memory and assimilation to context in delayed matching to sample. *Psychology Science.* (In press.)

Elman, J. L. (2005). Connectionist models of cognitive development: Where next? *Trends in Cognitive Sciences, 9,* 111–117.

Emmerton, J. (2001). Bird's judgment of number and quantity. Retrieved January 2004, from http://www.pigeon.psy.tufts.edu/avc/emmerton/default.htm

Emmerton, J., & Delius, J. D. (1993). Beyond sensation: Visual cognition in pigeons. In H. P. Zeigler & H.-J. Bischof (Eds.), *Vision, brain, and behaviour in birds* (pp. 377–390). Cambridge, MA: MIT Press.

Engel, A. K., & Singer, W. (2001). Temporal binding and the neural correlates of sensory awareness. *Trends in Cognitive Sciences, 5,* 16–25.

Engel, A. K., Fries, P., & Singer, W. (2001). Dynamic predictions: Oscillations and synchrony in top-down processing. *Nature Reviews Neuroscience, 2,* 704–716.

Engelmann, K. (1984). *Leben und Verhalten unseres Hausgeflügels.* [Life and behaviour of our fowl.] Leipzig: Neumann.

Enquist, M., & Ghirlanda, S. (2005). *Neural networks and animal behaviour.* Princeton, NJ: Princeton University Press.

Epstein, W. (1977). Observations concerning the contemporary analysis of constancies. In W. Epstein (Ed.), *Stability and constancy in visual perception* (pp. 437–447). New York: Wiley.

Erlhagen, W. (2003). Internal models for visual perception. *Biological Cybernetics, 88,* 409–417.

Erlhagen, W., & Jahnke, D. (2004). The role of action planning and other cognitive factors in motion extrapolation: A modelling study. *Visual Cognition, 11,* 315–340.

Erlhagen, W., & Schöner, G. (2002). Dynamic field theory of movement preparation. *Psychological Review, 109,* 545–572.

Estes, W. K. (1983). Categorization, perception, and learning. In T. J. Tighe & B. E. Shepp (Eds.), *Perception, cognition, and development: Interactional analyses* (pp. 323–351). Hillsdale, NJ: Lawrence Erlbaum Associates, Inc.

Farid, H. (2002). Temporal synchrony in perceptual grouping: A critique. *Trends in Cognitive Sciences, 6,* 284–289.

Feigenson, L., Dehaene, S., & Spelke, E. (2004). Core systems of number. *Trends in Cognitive Science, 8,* 307–314.

Fraisse, P. (1984). Perception and estimation of time. *Annual Review of Psychology, 35,* 1–36.

Garner, W. R. (1954). Context effects and the validity of loudness scales. *Journal of Experimental Psychology, 48,* 218–224.

Gauthier, I., & Palmeri, T. J. (2002). Visual neurons: Categorization-based selectivity. *Current Biology, 2,* R282–R284.

Gazzaniga, M. S. (Ed.). (2000). *The new cognitive neurosciences.* (2nd ed.). Cambridge, MA: MIT Press. (3rd ed. 2004.)

Gescheider, G. A. (1985). *Psychophysics: Method, theory, and application* (2nd ed.). Hillsdale, NJ: Lawrence Erlbaum Associates, Inc.

Gescheider, G. A. (1988). Psychophysical scaling. *Annual Review of Psychology, 39,* 169–200.

Ghirlanda, S. (2002). Intensity generalization: Physiology and modelling of a neglected topic. *Journal of Theoretical Biology, 214,* 389–404.

Ghirlanda, S., & Enquist, M. (2003). One century of generalization. *Animal Behaviour*, *66*, 15–36.

Gibson, E. J. (1983). Commentary on the development of perception and cognition. In T. J. Tighe & B. E. Shepp (Eds.), *Perception, cognition, and development: Interactional analyses* (pp. 307–321). Hillsdale, NJ: Lawrence Erlbaum Associates, Inc.

Gibson, E. J. (1991). *An odyssey in learning and perception*. Cambridge, MA: MIT Press.

Gibson, E. J., & Pick, A. (2000). *An ecological approach to perceptual learning and development*. New York: Oxford University Press.

Gierlatzek, B. (1985). *Entwicklungspsychologische Experimente zur Urteilsstabilität*. [Developmental studies on judgemental stability.] Königstein, Germany: Hain.

Gilbert, C. D., & Wiesel, T. N. (1990). The influence of contextual stimuli on the orientation selectivity of cells in primary visual cortex of the cat. *Vision Research*, *30*, 1689–1701.

Gilchrist, A. L. (1990). Developments in the Gestalt theory of lightness perception. In I. Rock (Ed.), *The legacy of Solomon Asch: Essays in cognition and social psychology* (pp. 213–232). Hillsdale, NJ: Lawrence Erlbaum Associates, Inc.

Gilchrist, A. L. (1994). Introduction: Absolute versus relative theories of lightness perception. In A. L. Gilchrist (Ed.), *Lightness, brightness, and transparency* (pp. 1–34). Hillsdale, NJ: Lawrence Erlbaum Associates, Inc.

Gilchrist, A. L., & Bonato, F. (1995). Anchoring of lightness values in center-surround displays. *Journal of Experimental Psychology: Human Perception and Performance*, *21*, 1437–1440.

Girgus, J. S., Coren, S., & Fraenkel, R. (1975). Levels of perceptual processing in the development of the visual illusions. *Developmental Psychology*, *11*, 268–273.

Gogel, W. C. (1972). Depth adjacency and cue effectiveness. *Journal of Experimental Psychology*, *77*, 176–181.

Gogel, W. C. (1977). The metric of visual space. In W. Epstein (Ed.), *Stability and constancy in visual perception* (pp. 129–181). New York: Wiley.

Gogel, W. C. (1998). An analysis of perceptions from changes in optical size. *Perception and Psychophysics*, *60*, 805–820.

Gold, I. (2003). Philosophy of neuroscience. In L. Nadel (Ed.), *Encyclopedia of cognitive science* (Vol. 3, pp. 606–612). New York: Nature.

Goldman-Rakic, P. S. (1988). Topography of cognition: Parallel distributed networks in primate association cortex. *Annual Review of Neuroscience*, *11*, 137–156.

Goldstone, R. L. (2003). Learning to perceive while perceiving to learn. In R. Kimchi, M. Behrmann, & C. R. Olson (Eds.), *Perceptual organization in vision: Behavioral and neural perspectives* (pp. 233–278). Mahwah, NJ: Lawrence Erlbaum Associates, Inc.

Gomez, J.-C. (2005). Species comparative studies and cognitive development. *Trends in Cognitive Sciences*, *9*, 118–125.

Gottlieb, G. (1998). Normally occurring environmental and behavioral influences on gene activity: From central dogma to probabilistic epigenesis. *Psychological Review*, *105*, 792–802.

Gottlieb, G. (2002). *Individual development and evolution: The genesis of novel behavior*. New York: Oxford University Press.

Gottlieb, G., & Krasnegor, N. A. (Eds.). (1985). *Measurement of audition and vision in the first year of postnatal life: A methodological overview*. Norwood, NJ: Ablex.

Gottlieb, G., & Krasnegor, N. A. (1985). Epilogue. In G. Gottlieb & N. A. Krasnegor (Eds.), *Measurement of audition and vision in the first year of postnatal life: A methodological overview* (pp. 455–456). Norwood, NJ: Ablex.

Gould, J. L. (2002). Can honey bees create cognitive maps? In M. Bekoff, C. Allen, & G. M. Burghardt (Eds.), *The cognitive animal: Empirical and theoretical perspectives on animal cognition* (pp. 41–46). Cambridge, MA: MIT Press.

Green, D. M., & Swets, J. A. (1966). *Signal detection theory and psychophysics.* New York: Wiley.

Gregory, R. L. (2003). Illusions. In L. Nadel (Ed.), *Encyclopedia of cognitive science.* (Vol. 2, pp. 460–466). New York: Nature.

Gregson, R. A. M. (1975). *Psychometrics of similarity.* New York: Academic Press.

Gregson, R. A. M. (1988). *Nonlinear psychophysical dynamics.* Hillsdale, NJ: Lawrence Erlbaum Associates, Inc.

Gregson, R. A. M. (1992) *N-dimensional nonlinear psychophysics: Theory and case studies.* Hillsdale, NJ: Lawrence Erlbaum Associates, Inc.

Gregson, R. A. M. (1995). *Cascades and fields in perceptual psychophysics.* Singapore: Worlds Scientific Publ.

Gregson, R. A. M. & Sarris, V. (1985, 5 September). The mathematics of psychophysical "frames of reference". Unpublished manuscript, J. W. Goethe University, Institute of Psychology, Frankfurt/M.

Grondin, S. (2001). From physical time to the first and second moments of psychological time. *Psychological Bulletin, 127,* 22–44.

Grossberg, S. (1999). How does the cerebral cortex work? Learning, attention, and grouping by the laminar circuits of visual cortex. *Spatial Vision, 12,* 163–187.

Grossberg, S. (2000). The complementary brain: Unifying brain dynamics and modularity. *Trends in Cognitive Sciences, 4,* 233–246.

Haber, R. N., & Hershenson, M. (1973). *The psychology of visual perception.* New York: Holt, Rinehart & Winston.

Hahn, D. (2003). Similarity. In L. Nadel (Ed.), *Encyclopedia of cognitive science* (Vol. 4, pp. 1–4). New York: Nature.

Hamada, J., Ehrenstein, W. H., & Paramei, G. V. (2003). Size assimilation and attention. *Perception, 32 Suppl.,* 135–136.

Hamburger, K., Prior, H., Sarris, V., & Spillmann, L. (2005). Filling-in with colour: Different modes of surface completion. *Vision Research.* (In press.)

Haubensak, G. (1992). The consistency model: A process model for absolute judgments. *Journal of Experimental Psychology: Human Perception and Performance, 18,* 303–309.

Haubensak, G., & Petzold, P. (2002). Influence of instructions on category rating. *Perception and Psychophysics, 64,* 325–338.

Hauf, P. (2001). *Untersuchungen zum altersspezifischen mehrdimensionalen perzeptiv-kognitiven Urteilsverhalten in der Psychophysik.* [Experiments on age-specific multidimensional perceptual cognitive behaviour in psychophysics.] In F. Wilkening, O. Güntürkün, T. Rammsayer, V. Sarris, & F. Strack (Eds.), *Psychologia Universalis, Neue Reihe* (Bd. 26). Lengerich, Germany: Pabst.

Hauf, P., & Baillargeon, R. (2005). *Infants use weight information to guide their reaching.* (In preparation.)

Hauf, P., & Sarris, V. (1999, November). *Age-related development of multidimensional judgment strategies in psychophysics: Size, color and brightness dimensions combined.* Poster presented at the 40th Annual Meeting of the Psychonomic Society, Los Angeles, CA (Abstract).

Hauf, P., & Sarris, V. (2001a). *Multidimensional judgments in psychophysics: Size, color and brightness dimensions combined*. Poster for presentation at the 1st Vision Sciences Meeting, Sarasota, FL, USA.

Hauf, P., & Sarris, V. (2001b). The "four stimulus-two choice" paradigm in multi-dimensional psychophysics: Size, brightness, and color dimensions combined. In E. Sommerfeld, R. Kompass, & T. Lachmann (Eds.), *Fechner Day 2001: Proceedings of the 17th Annual Meeting of the International Society for Psychophysics* (pp. 409–414). Lengerich, Germany: Pabst.

Hauf, P., Sarris, V., & Prior, H. (2005). *Relational psychophysics in the infant chick*. (In preparation.)

Heidelberger, M. (2004). Fechner's (wider) conception of psychophysics – then and now. In A. M. Oliveira, M. Teixeira, G. F. Borges, & M. J. Ferro (Eds.), *Fechner Day 2004: Proceedings of the 20th Annual Meeting of the International Society for Psychophysics* (pp. 18–25). Coimbra, Portugal: ISP.

Heinemann, E. (1983). The presolution period and the detection of statistical associations. In M. L. Commons, R. J. Herrnstein, & A. R. Wagner (Eds.), *Quantitative analyses of behavior: Computational and clinical approaches to pattern recognition and concept formation* (Vol. 4, pp. 21–35). Cambridge, MA: Ballinger.

Heinemann, E. (1997). Effects of various spatial transformations on pigeons' recognition of visual patterns: Some applications of the Heinemann-Chase pattern recognition model. In S. Watanabe & S. Chase (Eds.), *Pattern recognition in humans and animals* (pp. 1–10). Tokyo: Keio University Press.

Heinemann, E., & Chase, S. (1990). Memory limitations in human and animal signal detection. In J. A. Commons, J. A. Nevin, & M. C. Davison (Eds.), *Mechanisms, models and application of signal detection: Quantitative analysis of behavior* (pp. 17–28). Hillsdale, NJ: Lawrence Erlbaum Associates, Inc.

Heiss, B. (1984). *Kategorialleistungen von Kleinstkindern – ein experimenteller Beitrag zur Frage nach den Bedingungen für den Aufbau stabilen Urteilsverhaltens*. [Category building performance in human infants – an experimental account of the factors underlying the developmental stability of judgemental behaviour.] Frankfurt a.M.: Lang.

Hellström, A. (1985). The time-order error and its relatives: Mirrors of cognitive processes in comparing. *Psychological Bulletin, 97*, 35–61.

Helson, H. (1947). Adaptation-level as frame of reference for prediction of psychophysical data. *American Journal of Psychology, 60*, 1–29.

Helson, H. (1964). *Adaptation-level theory*. New York: Harper & Row.

Hertz, M. (1933). Über figurale Intensitäten und Qualitäten in der optischen Wahrnehmung der Biene. [On figural intensities and qualities in the bee's visual perception.] *Biologisches Zentralblatt, 53*, 10–40.

Hertz, M. (1934). Zur Physiologie des Formen- und Bewegungssehens: Optomotorische Versuche an Fliegen. [On the physiology of form and motion vision: opto-motor studies in flies.] *Zeitschrift für Vergleichende Physiologie, 20*, 430–449.

Hinson, J. M., & Lockhead, G. R. (1986). Range effects in successive discrimination. *Journal of Experimental Psychology: Animal Behavior Processes, 12*, 220–278.

Hinson, J. M., & Tennison, L. R. (1998). Range effects using instrumental choice procedures. *Animal Learning and Behavior, 26*, 60–75.

Hochstein, S., & Ahissar, M. (2002). View from the top: Hierarchies and reverse hierarchies in the visual system. *Neuron, 36*, 791–804.

Hofer, G. (1988). *Reizgeneralisation und Urteilskontext: Allgemein- und entwicklun-*

gspsychologische Untersuchungen zur Wahrnehmungsrelativität beim Gewichteheben mit variabler Kategorienzahl. [Stimulus generalization and judgemental context: Age-specific studies of the perceptual relativity with variable number of rating categories.] Unpublished doctoral dissertation: Frankfurt University.

Hollingworth, H. L. (1910). The central tendency of judgment. *Journal of Philosophy, Psychology and Scientific Methods, 7*, 461 469.

Hommel, B. (2004). Event files: Feature binding in and across perception and action. *Trends in Cognitive Sciences, 8*, 494–500.

Honey, R. C., & Bolhuis, J. J. (1997). Imprinting, conditioning, and within-event learning. *Quarterly Journal of Experimental Psychology, 50B*, 97–110.

Honey, R. C., Horn, G., & Bateson, P. P. G. (1992). Perceptual learning during filial imprinting: Evidence from transfer of training studies. *Quarterly Journal of Experimental Psychology, 46B*, 253–269.

Howard, M. W. (2004). Scaling behaviour in the temporal context model. *Journal of Mathematical Psychology, 48*, 230–238.

Howard, M. W., Fotedar, M. S., Datey, A. V., & Hasselmo, M. E. (2005). The temporal context model in spatial navigation and relational learning: Toward a common explanation of medial temporal lobe function across domains. *Psychological Review, 110*, 75–116.

Hubel, D. H. (1995). Foreword. In T. V. Papathomas (Ed.), *Early vision and beyond* (pp. iii–v). Cambridge, MA: MIT Press.

Huber, L. (2001). *Visual categorization in pigeons.* Retrieved January 2004, from http://www.pigeon.psy.tufts.edu.avc/huber/default.htm

Hulse, S. H. & Cynx, J. (1985). Relative pitch perception is constrained by absolute pitch in songbirds (*Mimus, Molothus, and Sturnus*). *Journal of Comparative Psychology, 99*, 176–196.

Hulse, S. H., Page, S. C., & Braaten, R. F. (1990). An integrative approach to auditory perception by songbirds. In W. C. Stebbins & M. A. Berkley (Eds.), *Comparative perception: Vol.2, Complex signals* (pp. 3–34). New York: Wiley.

Hulse, S. H., Takeuchi, A. H., & Braaten, R. F. (1992). Perceptual invariances in the comparative psychology of music. *Music Perception, 10*, 151–184.

Hulse, S. H., MacDougall-Shackleton, S. A., & Wisniewski, A. B. (1997). Auditory scene analysis by songbirds: Stream segregation of birdsong by European starlings (*Stumus vulgaris*). *Journal of Comparative Psychology, 111*, 3–13.

Humphreys, G. W. (2003). Binding in vision as a multistage process. In R. Kimchi, M. Behrmann, & C. R. Olson (Eds.), *Perceptual organization in vision: Behavioral and neural perspectives* (pp. 377–402). Mahwah, NJ: Lawrence Erlbaum Associates, Inc.

Jacobs, D. W. (2003). Perceptual completion and memory. In R. Kimchi, N., M. Behrmann, & C. R. Olson (Eds.), *Perceptual organization in vision: Behavioral and neural perspectives* (pp. 403–430). Mahwah, NJ: Lawrence Erlbaum Associates, Inc.

Johnson, D. M. (1949a). Generalization of a reference scale for judging pitch. *Journal of Experimental Psychology, 39*, 316–321.

Johnson, D. M. (1949b). Learning function for a change in the scale of judgment. *Journal of Experimental Psychology, 39*, 851–860.

Johnson, M. H. (1999). Developmental cognitive neuroscience. In M. Bennett (Ed.), *Developmental psychology: Achievements and prospects* (pp. 147–164). Hove, UK: Psychology Press.

Johnson, M. H. (2005). *Developmental cognitive neuroscience: An introduction* (2nd ed.) Oxford: Blackwell. (1st ed., 1997.)

Johnson, M. H., & Munakata, Y. (2005). Cognitive development: at the crossroads? *Trends in Cognitive Sciences, 9*, 91–92.

Jones, L. A., & Wearden, J. H. (2004). Double standards: Memory loading in temporal reference memory. *Quarterly Journal of Experimental Psychology, 57B*, 55–57.

Kaernbach, C., Schröger, E., & Müller, H. (Eds.). (2004). *Psychophysics beyond sensation: Laws and invariants of human cognition.* Mahwah, NJ: Lawrence Erlbaum Associates, Inc.

Kanisza, G. (1994). Gestalt theory has been misinterpreted, but has also had some real conceptual difficulties. *Philosophical Psychology, 7*, 149–162.

Kanisza, G., Renzi, P., Conti, S., Compostella, C., & Guerani, L. (1993). Amodal completion in mouse vision. *Perception, 22*, 713–721.

Karmiloff-Smith, A. (1992). *Beyond modularity: A developmental perspective on cognitive science.* Cambridge, MA: MIT Press.

Kastner, S. (2004). A neural basis of human visual attention. In L. Chalupa & J. S. Werner (Eds.), *The Visual Neurosciences* (Vol. 2, pp. 1514–1523). Cambridge, MA: MIT Press.

Kellman, P. J. (2003). Visual perception of objects and boundaries: A four-dimensional approach. In R. Kimchi, M. Behrmann, & C. R. Olson (Eds.), *Perceptual organization in vision: Behavioral and neural perspectives* (pp. 155–201). Mahwah, NJ: Lawrence Erlbaum Associates, Inc.

Kendler, T. S. (1979). The development of discrimination learning: A levels-of-functioning explanation. In H. W. Reese & L. P. Lipsett (Eds.), *Advances in Child Development and Behavior, 13*, 83–117.

Kimchi, R. (1992). Primacy of wholistic processing and global/local paradigm: A critical review. *Psychological Bulletin, 112*, 24–38.

Kimchi, R. (1998). Uniform connectedness and grouping in the perceptual organization of hierarchical patterns. *Journal of Experimental Psychology: Human Perception and Performance, 24*, 1105–1118.

Klix, F. (2003). Evolutionary events imprint learning, concept formation, and language. *Zeitschrift für Psychologie, 102*, 2–18.

Koch, C. (2004). *The quest for consciousness: A neurobiological approach.* Englewood, CO: Roberts.

Koffka, K. (1922). Perception: An introduction to the Gestalt-Theorie. *Psychological Bulletin, 19*, 531–585.

Köhler, W. (1951). Relational determination in perception. In L. A. Jeffres (Ed.), *Cerebral mechanism in behavior* (pp. 200–230). New York: Wiley.

Kovacs, I. (1996). Gestalten of today: Early processing of visual contours and surfaces. *Behavioural Brain Research, 82*, 1–11.

Krantz, D. H. (1972). A theory of magnitude estimation and cross-modality matching. *Journal of Mathematical Psychology, 9*, 168–199.

Kressley-Mba, R. A. (2001). *The history of animal psychology in Germany as an antecedent to German comparative psychology and ethology prior to 1940 with special emphasis on nonhuman primates.* Unpublished doctoral dissertation, Passau University, Germany.

Kressley-Mba, R. A., & Jäger, S. (2003). Rediscovering a missing link: The sensory physiologist and comparative psychologist Mathilde Hertz (1891–1975). *History of Psychology, 6*, 379–396.

Kubovy, M. (2003). Psychological phenomenology. In L. Nadel (Ed.), *Encyclopedia of cognitive science* (Vol. 3, pp. 579–586). New York: Nature.

Kubovy, M., & Gepshtein, S. (2003). Perceptual grouping in space and time: An exercise in phenomenological psychophysics. In R. Kimchi, M. Behrmann, & C. R. Olson (Eds.), *Perceptual organization in vision: Behavioral and neural perspectives* (pp. 45–86). Mahwah, NJ: Lawrence Erlbaum Associates, Inc.

Laming, D. (1986). Psychophysics. In R. L. Gregory (Ed.), *The Oxford companion to the mind* (pp. 655–659). Oxford: Oxford University Press.

Laming, D. (1997). *The measurement of sensation*. Oxford: Oxford University Press.

Lazareva, O. F., Smirnova, A. A., Bacozkaja, M. S., Zorina, Z. A., Rayevsky, V. V., & Wasserman, E. A. (2005). Transitive responding in hooded crows requires linearly ordered stimuli. *Journal of the Experimental Analysis of Behavior, 82*, 1–19.

Lea, S. E. G. (1984). *Instinct, environment and behaviour*. London: Methuen.

Lea, S. E. G., Slater, A. M., & Ryan, C. M. E. (1996). Perception of object unity in chicks: Comparison with the human infant. *Infant Behaviour and Development, 19*, 501–504.

Lee, T. S. (2003). Neural basis of attentive perceptual organization. In R. Kimchi, M. Behrmann, & C. R. Olson (Eds.), *Perceptual organization in vision: Behavioral and neural perspectives* (pp. 431–458). Mahwah, NJ: Lawrence Erlbaum Associates, Inc.

Lefkowicz, D. J., & Lickliter, R. (1994). *The development of intersensory perception: Comparative perspectives*. Hillsdale, NJ: Lawrence Erlbaum Associates, Inc.

Levin, I., & Wilkening, F. (1989). Measuring time via counting: The development of children's conception of time as a quantifiable dimension. In I. Levin & D. Zakay (Eds.), *Time and human cognition: A life-span perspective* (pp. 119–144). North-Holland: Elsevier.

Levine, M. J. (2003). Explanatory gap. In L. Nadel (Ed.), *Encyclopaedia of cognitive science* (Vol. 1, pp. 86–91). New York: Nature.

Lickliter, R., & Bahrick, L. E. (2000). The development of infant intersensory perception: Advantages of a comparative convergent-operations approach. *Psychological Bulletin, 126*, 260–280.

Lickliter, R., Bahrick, L. E., & Honeycutt, H. H. (2002). Intersensory redundancy facilitated prenatal perceptual learning in bobwhite quail embryos. *Developmental Psychology, 38*, 15–23.

Link, S. W. (1992). *The wave theory of difference and similarity*. Hillsdale, NJ: Lawrence Erlbaum Associates, Inc.

Link, S. (2003). Gustav Theodor Fechner. In L. Nadel (Ed.), *Encyclopedia of cognitive science* (Vol. 2, pp. 126–129). New York: Nature.

Link, S. W. (2004). Discussion ["The Sarris effect"]. In A. M. Oliveira, M. Teixeira, G. F. Borges, & M. J. Ferro (Eds.), *Fechner Day 2004: Proceedings of the 20th Annual Meeting of the International Society for Psychophysics* (pp. 184–189). Coimbra, Portugal: ISP.

Lockhead, G. R. (1992). Psychophysical scaling: Judgments of attributes or objects? *Behavioral and Brain Sciences, 15*, 543–601.

Lockhead, G. R. (2004). Absolute judgments are relative: A reinterpretation of some psychophysical ideas. *Review of General Psychology, 8*, 265–272.

Lockhead, G. R., & Hinson, J. (1986). Range and sequence effects in judgment. *Perception and Psychophysics, 40*, 53–61.

Lorenz, K. (1935). Der Kumpan in der Umwelt des Vogels. [The companion in the bird's world.] *Journal für Ornithologie, 83*, 137–213, 289–413.

Lorenz, K. (1958). The evolution of behaviour. *Scientific American, 199*, 219–268.

Lu, Z.-L., & Dosher, B. A. (2000). Spatial attention: Different mechanisms for central and peripheral temporal precues? *Journal of Experimental Psychology: Human Perception and Performance, 26,* 1534–1548.

Lu, Z.-L., & Sperling, G. (1996). Three systems for visual motion perception. *Current Directions in Psychological Science, 5,* 44–53.

Lu, Z.-L., & Sperling, G. (2001). Three-systems theory of human visual motion update. *Journal of the Optical Society of America, 18,* 2331–2370.

Lu, Z.-L., & Sperling (2002). Stereomotion is processed by the third-order motion system: Reply to comment. *Journal of the Optical Society of America, A19,* 2144–2153.

Lu, Z.-L., Jeon, S.-T., & Dosher, B. A. (2004). Temporal tuning characteristics of the perceptual template and endogeneous cuing of spatial attention. *Vision Research, 44,* 1333–1350.

Luce, D. R. (2004). Guest editorial. In C. Kaernbach, E. Schröger, & H. Müller (Eds.), *Psychophysics beyond sensation: Laws and invariants of human cognition* (pp. 3–7). Mahwah, NJ: Lawrence Erlbaum Associates, Inc.

Mackintosh, N. J., Wilson, B., & Boakes, R. A. (1985). Differences in mechanisms of intelligence among vertebrates. *Philosophical Transaction of the Royal Society of London Series, B308,* 53–65. (Quoted after Pearce, 1994.)

Maddox, W. T. (2002). Learning and attention in multidimensional identification and categorization: Separating low-level processes and high-level decisional processes. *Journal of Experimental Psychology: Learning, Memory and Cognition, 28,* 99–115.

Mandler, J. M. (2000). Perceptual and conceptual processes in [human] infancy. *Journal of Cognition and Development, 1,* 3–36.

Mandler, J. M. (2004). Thought before language. *Trends in Cognitive Sciences, 8,* 508–513.

Markman, A. G., & Ross, B. H. (2003). Category use and category learning. *Psychological Bulletin, 129,* 592–613.

Marks, L. E., & Algom, D. (1998). Psychophysical scaling. In M. H. Birnbaum (Ed.), *Handbook of perception and cognition: Measurement, judgment, and decision making* (pp. 81–178). Mahwah, NJ: Lawrence Erlbaum Associates, Inc.

Marr, D. (1982). *Vision: A computational investigation into the human representation and processing of visual information.* San Francisco: Freeman.

Mausfeld, R. (2002). The physicalistic trap in perception theory. In D. Heyer & R. Mausfeld (Eds.), *Perception and the physical world: Psychological and philosophical issues in perception* (pp. 75–112). New York: Wiley.

Medin, D., Goldstone, R., & Gentner, D. (1993). Respects for similarity. *Psychological Review, 100,* 254–278.

Mellers, B. A., & Birnbaum, M. H. (1982). Loci of contextual effects in judgment. *Journal of Experimental Psychology: Human Perception and Performance, 8,* 582–601.

Metzger, W. (1929). Zur Phänomenologie des homogenen Ganzfeldes. [On the phenomenology of the homogenous Ganzfeld.] *Psychologische Forschung, 13,* 6–29.

Mori, S. (1998). Effects of stimulus information and number of stimuli on sequential dependencies in absolute identification. *Canadian Journal of Experimental Psychology, 52,* 72–83.

Mori, S., & Ward, L. M. (1995). Pure feedback effects in absolute identification. *Perception and Psychophysics, 57,* 1065–1079.

Morris, R. G. M. (1994). The neural basis of learning with particular reference to the role of synaptic plasticity: Where are we a century after Cajal's speculations? In

N. J. Mackintosh (Ed.), *Animal learning and cognition: Handbook of perception and cognition* (pp. 135–183). New York: Academic Press.

Murray, D. J. (1993). A perspective for viewing the history of psychophysics. *Behavioral and Brain Sciences, 16,* 115–186.

Murray, D. J. (1995). *Gestalt psychology and the cognitive revolution.* New York: Harvester Wheatsheaf.

Murray, D. J., & Bandomir, C. A. (2001). Fechner's inner psychophysics viewed from both a Herbertian and Fechnerian perspective. In E. Sommerfeld, R. Kompass, & T. Lachmann (Eds.), *Fechner Day 2001: Proceedings of the 17th Annual Meeting of the International Society for Psychophysics* (pp. 49–54). Lengerich, Germany: Pabst.

Mussweiler, T. (2003). Comparison processes in social judgement: Mechanisms and consequences. *Psychological Review, 110,* 472–489.

Nadel, L. (Ed.). (2003). *Encyclopedia of cognitive science* (4 Vols.) New York: Nature.

Nagel, T. (1974). What is it like to be a bat? *Philosophical Review, 82,* 435–450.

Nagel, T. (1995). *Other minds: Critical essays 1969–1994.* New York: Oxford University Press.

Nagel, T. (1997). *The last word.* New York: Oxford University Press.

Nakayama, K., Shimojo, S., & Ramachandran, V. S. (1990). Transparency: Relation to depth, subjective contours, luminance, and neon color spreading, *Perception, 19,* 497–513.

Namba, S., & Kuwano, S. (2000). The validity of scaling and subjective assessment of noise in relation to frame of reference. In A. Schick, M. Meis, & C. Reckhardt (Eds.), *Contributions to psychological acoustics* (pp. 15–38). Oldenburg, Germany: University of Oldenburg Press.

Neumeyer, C. (1991). Evolution of colour vision. In J. Cronly-Dillon (Ed.), *Vision and visual dysfunction* (Vol. 2, pp. 284–305). Basingstoke: Macmillan.

Neumeyer, C. (1998). Comparative aspects of color constancy. In V. Walsh & J. Kulikowski (Eds.), *Perceptual constancy: Why things look as they do* (pp. 323–351). Cambridge: Cambridge University Press.

Nieder, A. (2002). Seeing more than meets the eye: Processing of illusory contours in animals. *Journal of Comparative Physiology A, 188,* 249–260.

Norris, C. (1997). *Against relativism: Philosophy of science, deconstruction, and critical theory.* Oxford: Blackwell.

Norwich, K. H. (1993). *Information, sensation, and perception.* San Diego, CA: Academic Press.

Nosofsky, R. M. (1986). Attention, similarity, and the identification/categorization relationship. *Journal of Experimental Psychology: General, 115,* 39–57.

Nosofsky, R. M. (1992). Similarity scaling and cognitive process models. *Annual Review of Psychology, 43,* 25–53.

Nosofsky, R. M. (1997). An exemplar-based random-walk model of speeded categorization and absolute judgment. In A. A. J. Marley (Ed.), *Choice, decision, and measurement: Essays in honor of R. Duncan Luce* (pp. 347–365). Mahwah, NJ: Lawrence Erlbaum Associates, Inc.

Oliveira, A. M., Teixeira, M., Borges, G. F., & Ferro, M. J. (Eds.). (2004). *Fechner Day 2004: Proceedings of the 20th Annual Meeting of the International Society for Psychophysics.* Coimbra, Portugal: ISP.

O'Reilly, R., & Johnson, M. H. (1994). Object recognition and sensitive periods: A computational analysis of visual imprinting. *Neural Computation, 6,* 357–390.

Oyama, T. (1959). A new psychophysical method: Method of transposition or equal-appearing relations. *Psychological Bulletin, 56*, 74–79.

Oyama, T. (1977). Analysis of causal relations in the perceptual constancies. In W. Epstein (Ed.), *Stability and constancy in visual perception* (pp. 183–216). New York: Wiley.

Palmer, S. E. (2003). Perceptual organization and grouping. In R. Kimchi, M. Behrmann, & C. R. Olson (Eds.), *Perceptual organization in vision: Behavioral and neural perspectives* (pp. 3–44). Mahwah. NJ: Lawrence Erlbaum Associates, Inc.

Papini, M. R. (2002). Pattern and process in the evolution of learning. *Psychological Review, 109*, 186–201.

Parducci, A. (1965). Category judgment: A range-frequency model. *Psychological Review, 72*, 407–418.

Parducci, A. (1982). Scale values and phenomenal experience: There is no psychophysical law! In H. G. Geissler, P. Petzold, H. G. J. M. Buffart, & Y. M. Zabrodin (Eds.), *Psychophysical judgment and the process of perception* (pp. 11–16). Berlin: VEB Deutscher Verlag der Wissenschaften.

Parducci, A. (1983). Category ratings and the relational character of judgment. In H.-G. Geissler, H. F. J. M. Buffart, E. L. Leeuwenberg, & V. Sarris (Eds.), *Modern issues in perception* (pp. 262–282). Berlin: Deutscher Verlag der Wissenschaften.

Parducci, A. (1995). *Happiness, pleasure, and judgment: The contextual theory and its applications.* Hillsdale, NJ: Lawrence Erlbaum Associates, Inc.

Parducci, A. (2004). Discussion ["The Sarris effect"]. In A. M. Oliveira, M. Teixeira, G. F. Borges, & M. J. Ferro (Eds.), *Fechner Day 2000: Proceedings of the 20th Annual Meeting of the International Society for Psychophysics* (pp. 184–189). Coimbra, Portugal: ISP.

Parducci, A., Knobel, S., & Thomas, R. (1976). Independent contexts for category ratings: A range-frequency analysis. *Perception and Psychophysics, 20*, 360–366.

Parker, S. (2002). Comparative development, evolutionary psychology and cognitive ethology: Contrasting but compatible research programs. In M. Bekoff, C. Allen, & M. G. Burghardt (Eds.), *The cognitive animal: Empirical and theoretical perspectives of animal cognition* (pp. 59–68). Cambridge, MA: MIT Press.

Parker, S., & Schneider, B. A. (1994). The stimulus range effect: Evidence for top-down control of sensory intensity in audition. *Perception and Psychophysics, 56*, 1–11.

Parovel, G., & Vezziani, S. (2002). Mirror symmetry opposes splitting of chromatically homogeneous surfaces. *Perception, 31*, 681–709.

Pasternak, T., & Greenlee, M. W. (2005). *Nature reviews neuroscience.* Retrieved 14 January, 2005, from www.nature.com/reviews/neuro

Pearce, J. M. (1994). Discrimination and categorization. In N. J. Mackintosh (Ed.), *Animal learning and cognition: Handbook of perception and cognition* (pp. 109–134). New York: Academic Press.

Pessoa, L., Thompson, E., & Noe, A. (1998). Finding out about fitting-in: A guide to perceptual completion for visual science and the philosophy of perception. *Behavioral and Brain Sciences, 21*, 723–748.

Peterhans, E., & von der Heydt, R. (1991). Subjective contours – bridging the gap between psychophysics and physiology. *Trends in Neuroscience, 14*, 112–119.

Peterson, M. A. (1999). Top-down influences on distinctly perceptual processes. *Behavioral and Brain Sciences, 22*, 389–390.

Peterson, M. A. (2003). Vision: Top-down effects. In L. Nadel (Ed.), *The encyclopedia of cognitive science* (Vol. 4, pp. 500–504). New York: Nature.

Petrov, A. A., & Anderson, J. R. (2005). The dynamic of scaling: A memory-based anchor model of category-rating and absolute identification. *Psychological Review*, *112*, 383–416.

Petrusic, W. M. (2001). Contextual effects and associative processes in comparative judgements with perceptual and symbolic stimuli. In E. Sommerfeld, R. Kompass, & T. Lachmann (Eds.), *Fechner Day 2001: Proceedings of the 17th Meeting of the International Society for Psychophysics* (pp. 75–80). Lengerich, Germany: Pabst.

Petrusic, W. M. (2003). Calibration of response times and confidence in perception and cognition. In B. Berglund & E. Borg (Eds.), *Fechner Day 2003: Proceedings of the 19th Annual Meeting of the International Society for Psychophysics* (pp. 235–240). Stockholm: ISP.

Petzold, P., & Haubensak, G. (2004). Short-term and long-term frames of reference in category judgments: A multiple-standards model. In C. Kaernbach, E. Schröger, & H. Müller (Eds.), *Psychophysics beyond sensation: Laws and invariants of human cognition* (pp. 45–68). Mahwah, NJ: Lawrence Erlbaum Associates, Inc.

Piaget, J. (1969). *The mechanisms of perception*. London: Routledge & Kegan Paul.

Piaget, J. (1973). *Le développement de la notion de temps chez l'enfant*. Paris: Presses Universitaires de France. (Quoted after Zur Oeveste, 1987.)

Pick, H. L. (1983). Some issues on the relation between perceptual and cognitive development. In T. J. Tighe & B. E. Shepp (Eds.), *Perception, cognition, and development: Interactional analyses* (pp. 293–306). Hillsdale, NJ: Lawrence Erlbaum Associates, Inc.

Plotkin, H. (2004). *Evolutionary thought in psychology: A brief history*. Malden, MA: Blackwell.

Poggio, T. (2004). Q & A (Interview). *Current Biology*, *14*, 985–986.

Pomerantz, J. R., Portillo, M. C., Jewell, S. W., & Agrawal, A. (2003, November). *The genesis of perceptual organization: Basic emergent features in vision*. Paper presented at the 44th annual meeting of the Psychonomic Society, Vancouver, Canada.

Popper, K. R. (1998). *The world of Parmenides*. London: Routledge. (German translation, 2001.)

Poulton, E. C. (1989). *Bias in quantifying judgment*. Hove, UK: Lawrence Erlbaum Associates Ltd.

Putnam, H. (1988). *Representation and reality*. Cambridge, MA: MIT Press.

Quin, F. T., & Von der Heydt, R. (2005) Figure and ground in the visual cortex: V2 combines stereosco stereoscopic cues with gestalt rules. *Neuron, 47*, 155–166.

Quinlan, P. T., & Wilten, R. N. (1998). Grouping by proximity or similarity? Competition between the Gestalt principles in vision. *Perception*, *27*, 417–430.

Ranganath, C., & Blumenfeld, R. W. (2005). Doubts about double dissociations between short- and long-term memory. *Trends in Cognitive Sciences*, *9*, 374–380.

Ranganath, C., & D'Esposito, M. (2005). Directing the mind's eye: Prefontal, inferior and medial temporal mechanisms for visual working memory. *Current Opinion in Neurobiology*, *15*, 175–182.

Reese, H. W. (1968). *The perception of stimulus relations: Discrimination learning and transposition*. New York: Academic Press.

Regolin, L., & Vallortigara, G. (1995). Perception of partly occluded objects by young chicks. *Perception and Psychophysics*, *57*, 971–976.

Regolin, L., & Vallortigara, G. (2003). Aspects of visual perception and cognition in the avian brain. In B. Berglund & E. Borg (Eds.), *Fechner Day 2003: Proceedings of the 19th Annual Meeting of the International Society for Psychophysics* (pp. 245–250). Stockholm: ISP.

Regolin, L., Tommasi, L., & Vallortigara, G. (2000). Visual perception of biological motion in newly hatched chicks as revealed by an imprinting procedure. *Animal Cognition*, *3*, 53–67.

Rescorla, R. A. (2003). Elements and configural encoding of the conditioned stimulus. *Quarterly Journal of Experimental Psychology*, *56B*, 161–176.

Restle, F. (1978). Assimilation predicted by adaptation-level theory with variable weights. In N. J. Castellan & F. Restle (Eds.), *Cognitive theory*, (Vol 3, pp. 75–91). Hillsdale, NJ: Lawrence Erlbaum Associates, Inc.

Restle, F., & Merryman, C. T. (1968). An adaptation-level theory account of a relative-size illusion. *Psychonomic Science*, *12*, 229–230.

Restle, F., & Merryman, C. T. (1969). Distance and an illusion of line. *Journal of Experimental Psychology*, *81*, 297–302.

Richelle, M., & Lejeune, H. (1990). *Time and animal behaviour*. Oxford: Pergamon.

Riley, D. A. (1968). *Discrimination learning*. Boston: Allyn & Bacon.

Riley, D. A. and Langley, C. M. (1993). The logic of species comparisons. *Psychological Science*, *4*, 185–189.

Rock, I. (1977). In defense of unconscious inference. In W. Epstein (Ed.), *Stability and constancy in visual perception: Mechanisms and processes* (pp. 321–373). New York: Wiley.

Rock, I. (1990). The frame of reference. In I. Rock (Ed.), *The legacy of Solomon Asch: Essays in cognition and social psychology* (pp. 243–268). Hillsdale, NJ: Lawrence Erlbaum Associates, Inc.

Rock, I. (1996). *Indirect perception*. Cambridge, MA: MIT Press.

Rogers, L. J. (1995). *The development of brain and behaviour in the chicken*. Wallingford, Australia: CAB International.

Rookes, P., & Willson, J. (2000). *Perception: Theory, development and organization*. London: Routledge.

Rorty, R. (1991). *Objectivity, relativism, and truth*. Cambridge, MA: Cambridge University Press.

Rovee-Collier, C., & Barr, R. (2001). Infant learning and memory. In G. Bremner & A. Fogel (Eds.), *Blackwell handbook of infant development* (pp. 99–138). Oxford: Blackwell.

Rovee-Collier, C., Hayne, H., & Colombo, M. (2001). *The development of implicit and explicit memory.* (*Advances in consciousness research, Vol. 24.*) Amsterdam: Benjamins.

Rumbaugh, D. M., & Beran, M. J. (2003). Language acquisition by animals. In L. Nadel (Ed.), *Encyclopedia of cognitive science* (Vol. 2, pp. 700–730). New York: Nature.

Ryan, J. D., & Cohen, N. J. (2004). Processing and short-term retention of relational information in amnesia. *Neuropsychologia*, *42*, 497–511.

Sander, K. (1998). Das "Two-Stimulus Two-Choice"-Paradima für die Psychophysik: Range-Frequency-Modell und Adaptationsniveau-Theorie im Vergleich. [The two-stimulus two-choice paradigm in psychophysics: Range-frequency model and adaptation-level theory compared.] Marburg, Germany: Tectum. (Quoted after Sarris, 2004.)

Sander, K., & Sarris, V. (1997). Das "Two-Stimulus two-Choice"-Paradigma für die Psychophysik: Range-Frequency-Modell und Adaptation-Level-Theorie im Vergleich. [The two-stimulus two choice paradigm in psychophysics: Range-frequency model and adaptation-level theory compared.] *Zeitschrift für Experimentelle Psychologie, 44*, 431–446.

Sarris, V. (1967). Adaptation-level theory: Two critical experiments on Helson's weighted-average model. *American Journal of Psychology, 80*, 331–344.

Sarris, V. (1975). *Wahrnehmung und Urteil: Bezugssystemeffekte in der Psychophysik.* [Perception and judgment: Frame-of-reference effects in psychophysics.] (2nd. ed.) Göttingen, Germany: Hogrefe. (1st ed., 1971.)

Sarris, V. (1976). Effects of stimulus range and anchor value on psychophysical judgment. In H.-G. Geissler & Y. M. Zabrodin (Eds.), *Advances in psychophysics* (pp. 253–268). Berlin: Deutscher Verlag der Wissenschaften.

Sarris, V. (1984). On perceptual learning in geometrical-optical illusions. *Studia Psychologica (Bratislava), 26*, 29–37.

Sarris, V. (1986). Hermann Ebbinghaus' law of relative size-contrast in optico-geometric distortions: Rediscovery and reformulation. In F. Klix & H. Hagendorf (Eds.), *Human memory and cognitive capabilities* (pp. 139–151). Amsterdam: North-Holland.

Sarris, V. (1990). Contextual effects in animal psychophysics: A comparative analysis of the chicken's perceptual relativity. *European Bulletin of Cognitive Psychology, 10*, 475–489.

Sarris, V. (1994). Contextual effects in animal psychophysics: Comparative perception. *Behavioral and Brain Sciences, 17*, 763–764.

Sarris, V. (1995). *Max Wertheimer in Frankfurt*. Lengerich, Germany: Pabst.

Sarris, V. (1998). Frames-of-reference effects in psychophysics: New experimental findings with baby chicks. *Psychologia (Greece), 5*, 95–102.

Sarris, V. (2000). The bird's visual psychophysics: A perceptual-cognitive perspective. In C. Bonnet (Ed.), *Fechner Day 2000: Proceedings of the 16th Annual Meeting of the International Society for Psychophysics* (pp. 47–52). Strasbourg: ISP.

Sarris, V. (2001a). Frame-of-reference conceptions and context effects in psychophysics. In E. Sommerfeld, R. Kompass, & T. Lachmann (Eds.), *Fechner Day 2001: Proceedings of the 17th Meeting of the International Society for Psychophysics* (pp. 155–160). Lengerich, Germany: Pabst.

Sarris, V. (2001b). Wolfgang Köhler (1887–1967). In P. B. Baltes & N. J. Smelser (Eds.), *The encyclopedia of the social and behavioural sciences* (pp. 8155–8159). Oxford: Elsevier.

Sarris, V. (2004). Frame of reference models in psychophysics: A perceptual-cognitive approach. In C. Kaernbach, E. Schröger, & H. Müller (Eds.), *Psychophysics beyond sensation: Laws and invariants of human cognition* (pp. 69–88). Mahwah. NJ: Lawrence Erlbaum Associates, Inc.

Sarris, V. (2006). Bridging the gap between Gestalt psychology and psychophysics. In K. Noguchi (Ed.), *Psychology of beauty and Kansei: New horizons of Gestalt perception*. Tokyo: Fuzanbou International Press.

Sarris, V., & Haider, M. (1970). Average evoked potentials and pitch judgments. *Psychonomic Science, 20*, 113–115.

Sarris, V., & Parducci, A. (1978). Multiple anchoring of the neutral point of category rating scales. *Perception and Psychophysics, 24*, 35–39.

Sarris, V., & Schnehage-Poci, J. (2004). Comparative psychophysics: Putting the stimulus "range" into context. In A. M. Oliveira, M. Teixeira, G. F. Borges, &

M. J. Ferro (Eds.), *Fechner Day 2004: Proceedings of the 20th Annual Meeting of the International Society for Psychophysics* (pp. 184–189). Coimbra, Portugal: ISP.

Sarris, V., & Zoeke, B. (1985). Tests of a quantitative frame-of-reference model: Practice effects in psychophysical judgments with different age-groups. In G. d'Ydewalle (Ed.), *Cognition, information processing, and motivation* (pp. 71–78). Amsterdam: North-Holland.

Sarris, V., Hofer, G., & Zoeke, B. (1990). The chicken's visual psychophysics: Two-dimensional effects. In F. Müller (Ed.), *Fechner Day 1990: Proceedings of the 6th Annual Meeting of the International Society for Psychophysics* (pp. 222–227). Würzburg: Würzburg University Press.

Sarris, V., Hauf, P., & Arlt, M. (2001). The animal psychophysics of "relative" stimulus discrimination: Colour and size data from the baby chick. In E. Sommerfeld, R. Kompass, & T. Lachmann (Eds.), *Fechner Day 2001: Proceedings of the 17th Annual Meeting of the International Society for Psychophysics* (pp. 576–581). Lengerich, Germany: Pabst.

Schnehage-Poci, J., & Sarris, V. (2004), Zeitwahrnehmung und Zeitschätzung. [Time perception and time estimation.] *46. Tagung experimentell arbeitender Psychologen*; Giessen, 4–7 April (p. 232). Lengerich, Germany: Pabst.

Schneider, B. A., & Trehub, S. E. (1985). Infant auditory psychophysics: An overview. In G. Gottlieb & N. A. Krasnegor (Eds.), *Measurement of audition and vision in the first year of postnatal life* (pp. 127–155). Norwood, NJ: Ablex.

Sell, A., Hagen, E. H., Cosmides, L., & Tooby, J. (2003). Evolutionary psychology: Applications and criticisms. In L. Nadel (Ed.), *The encyclopaedia of cognitive science* (Vol. 2, pp. 47–53). New York: Nature.

Shepard, R. M. (1974). Representation of structure in similarity data: Problems and prospects. *Psychometrika*, *39*, 373–421.

Shepard, R. M. (1978). On the status of "direct" psychophysical measurement. In C. W. Savage (Ed.), *Minnesota studies in the philosophy of science: Issues in the foundations of psychology* (pp. 441–490). Minneapolis, MI: University of Minnesota Press.

Shepard, R. N. (1981a). Psychological relations and psychophysical scales: On the status of "direct" psychophysical measurement. *Journal of Mathematical Psychology*, *24*, 21–57.

Shepard, R. N. (1981b). Psychophysical complementarity. In M. Kubovy & J. R. Pomerantz (Eds.), *Perceptual organization* (pp. 279–341). Hillsdale, NJ: Lawrence Erlbaum Associates, Inc.

Shepard, R. N. (1987). Toward a universal law of generalization for psychological science. *Science*, *237*, 1317–1323.

Shepard, R. N. (2001). Perceptual-cognitive universals as reflections of the world. *Behavioral and Brain Sciences*, *24*, 581–601.

Siemann, M., & Delius, J. D. (1998). Algebraic learning and neural network models for transitive and non-transitive responding. *European Journal of Cognitive Psychology*, *18*, 307–334.

Singer, W. (1999). Neuronal synchrony: A versatile code for the definition of relations? *Neurons*, *24*, 49–65.

Singer, W. (2004). Synchrony, oscillations, and the relational codes. In M. L. Chalupa & J. S. Werner (Eds.), *The visual neurosciences* (Vol. 2, pp. 704–716). Cambridge, MA: MIT Press.

Slater, A. (1998). Visual organization and perceptual constancies in early infancy. In

V. Walsh & J. Kulikowski (Eds.), *Perceptual constancy: Why things look as they do* (pp. 6–30). Cambridge: Cambridge University Press.

Slater, A. (Ed.). (1998). *Perceptual development: Visual, auditory, and speech perception in infancy*. Hove, UK: Psychology Press.

Slater, A. (2001). Visual perception. In G. Bremner & A. Fogel (Eds.), *Blackwell handbook of infant development* (pp. 5–34). Oxford. Blackwell.

Sokolov, A., Pavlova, M., & Ehrenstein, W. H. (2000). Primacy and frequency effects in absolute judgments of visual velocity. *Perception and Psychophysics, 62*, 998–1007.

Solan, Z., & Ruppin, E. (2001). Similarity in perception: A window to brain organization. *Journal of Cognitive Neuroscience, 13*, 18–30.

Sommerfeld, E., Kompass, R., & Lachmann, T. (Eds.). (2001). *Fechner Day 2001: Proceedings of the 17th Annual Meeting of the International Society for Psychophysics*. Lengerich, Germany: Pabst.

Spelke, E. S. (1998). Nativism, empiricism, and the origins of knowledge. *Infant Behavior and Development, 21*, 181–200.

Spence, K. W. (1937). The differential response in animals to stimuli varying within a single dimension. *Psychological Review, 44*, 430–444.

Spiker, C. C., & Cantor, J. H., (1983). Components in the hypothesis-testing strategies of young children. In T. J. Tighe & B. E. Shepp (Eds.), *Perception, cognition, and development: Interactional analyses* (pp. 163–201). Hillsdale, NJ: Lawrence Erlbaum Associates, Inc.

Spillmann, L. (2005). From perceptive fields to Gestalt. *Perception, 34*, 36.

Spillmann, L., & Dresp, B. (1995). Phenomena of illusory form: Can we bridge the gap between levels of explanation? *Perception, 24*, 1333–1364.

Spillmann, L., & De Weerd, P. (2003). Mechanisms of surface completion: Perceptual filling-in of texture. In L. Pessoa & P. De Weerd (Eds.), *Filling-in: From perceptual completion to cortical reorganization* (pp. 81–105). Oxford: Oxford University Press.

Spillmann, L., & Ehrenstein, W. H. (2004). Gestalt factors in the visual neurosciences. In L. M. Chalupa & J. S. Werner (Eds.), *The visual neurosciences* (pp. 1573–1589). Cambridge, MA: MIT Press.

Stebbins, W. C. (Ed.). (1970). *Animal psychophysics: The design and conduct of sensory experiments*. New York: Appleton-Century-Crofts.

Stebbins, W. C. (1990). Perception in animal behavior. In M. A. Berkley & W. C. Stebbins (Eds.), *Comparative perception, Vol. I: Basic mechanisms* (pp. 1–26). New York: Wiley.

Stebbins, W. C. (1995). Uncertainty in the study of comparative perception: A methodological challenge. In M. Klump, R. J. Pooling, R. R. Fay, & W. C. Stebbins (Eds.), *Methods in comparative psychoacoustics* (pp. 331–342). Basel, Switzerland: Birkhäuser.

Stevens, S. S. (1958). Adaptation-level theory vs. the relativity of judgment. *American Journal of Psychology, 71*, 633–646.

Stevens, S. S. (1975). *Psychophysics: Introduction to its perceptual, neural, and social prospects*. New York: Wiley.

Stewart, N., & Brown, G. D. A. (2004). Sequence effects in the categorization of tones varying in frequency. *Journal of Experimental Psychology: Learning, Memory, and Cognition, 30*, 416–430.

Swets, J. A. (1996). *Signal detection theory and ROC analysis in psychology and diagnostics*. Mahwah, NJ: Lawrence Erlbaum Associates, Inc.

Tarr, M. J., & Bülthoff, H. H. (Eds.). (1998). *Object recognition in man, monkey, and machine*. Cambridge, MA: MIT Press.

Teghtsoonian, M., & Teghtsoonian, R. (1971). How repeatable are Stevens's power law exponents for individual subjects? *Perception and Psychophysics*, *10*, 147–149.

Teghtsoonian, M., & Teghtsoonian, R. (2003). Putting context effects into context. In B. Berglund & E. Borg (Eds.), *Fechner Day 2003: Proceedings of the 19th Annual Meeting of the International Society for Psychophysics* (pp. 309–314). Stockholm: ISP.

Teghtsoonian, R., & Teghtsoonian, M. (1997). Range of acceptable stimulus intensities: An estimator of dynamic range for intensive perceptual continua. *Perception and Psychophysics*, *59*, 721–728.

Teller, D. Y. (1983). Measurement of visual acuity in human and monkey infants: The interface between laboratory and clinic. *Behavioural and Brain Research*, *10*, 15–23.

Teller, D. Y. (1984). Linking proposition. *Vision Research*, *24*, 1233–1246.

Teller, D. Y. (1985). Psychophysics of infant vision: Definitions and limitations. In G. Gottlieb & N. A. Krasnegor (Eds.), *Measurement and audition in the first year of postnatal life: A methodological overview* (pp. 127–143). Norwood, NJ: Ablex.

Teller, D. Y. (2000). Visual development: Psychophysics, neural substrates, and causal stories. In M. S. Gazzaniga (Ed.), *The new cognitive neurosciences* (2nd ed., pp. 73–81). Cambridge, MA: MIT Press.

Thelen, E., & Smith, L. B. (1994). *A dynamic system approach to the development of cognition and action*. Cambridge, MA: MIT Press.

Thomas, D. R. (1993). A model for adaptation-level effects on stimulus generalization. *Psychological Review*, *100*, 658–673.

Thomas, D. R., Mood, K., Morrison, S., & Wiertelak, E. (1991). Peak shift revisited: A test of alternative interpretations. *Journal of Experimental Psychology: Animal Behavior Processes*, *17*, 130–140.

Tighe, T. J., & Shepp, B. E. (Eds.). (1983). *Perception, cognition, and development: Interactional analyses*. Hillsdale, NJ: Lawrence Erlbaum Associates, Inc.

Tomasi, C. (2003). Early vision. In L. Nadel (Ed.), *The encyclopedia of cognitive science* (Vol. 4, pp. 465–472). New York: Nature.

Townsend, J. T., & Pomerantz, J. R. (2004). Configurality. In A. M. Oliveira, M. Teixeira, G. F. Borges, & M. J. Ferro (Eds.), *Fechner Day 2004: Proceedings of the 20th Annual Meeting of the International Society for Psychophysics* (pp. 52–55). Coimbra, Portugal: ISP.

Townsend, J. T., & Spencer-Smith, J. (2004). Two kinds of global perceptual separability and curvature. In C. Kaernbach, E. Schröger, & H. Müller (Eds.). *Psychophysics beyond sensation: Laws and invariants of human cognition* (pp. 89–112). Mahwah, NJ: Lawrence Erlbaum Associates, Inc.

Townsend, J. T., & Wenger, M. J. (2004). A theory of interactive parallel processing: New capacity measures and predictions for a response time inequality series. *Psychological Review*, *111*, 1003–1035.

Trehub, S. E. (1990). The perception of musical patterns by human infants: The provision of similar patterns by their parents. In M. A. Berkley & W. C. Stebbins (Eds.), *Comparative perception: Vol. I: Basic mechanisms* (pp. 429–459). New York: Wiley.

Trehub, S. E. (1993). The music listening skills of infants and young children. In T. J. Tighe & W. J. Dowling (Eds.), *Psychology and music* (pp. 161–176). Hillsdale, NJ: Lawrence Erlbaum Associates, Inc.

Trehub, S. E. (2003). The developmental origins of musicality. *Nature Neuroscience, 6,* 669–673.

Trehub, S. E., & Trainor, L. (1994). Listening strategies in infancy: The roots of language and musical development. In S. McAdams & E. Bigand (Eds.), *Cognitive aspects of human audition* (pp. 278–327). Oxford: Oxford University Press.

Tyler, C. W., & Chen, C.-C. (2000). Signal detection theory in the 2AFC paradigm: Attention, channel uncertainty and probability summation. *Vision Research, 40,* 3121–3144.

Urcuioli, P. J. (2003). Generalization. In L. Nadel (Ed.), *Encyclopedia of cognitive science* (Vol. 2, pp. 275–281). New York: Nature.

Ushitani, T., Fujita, K., & Yamanaka, R. (2001). Do pigeons (*Columba livia*) perceive object unity? *Animal Cognition, 4,* 153–161.

Uttal, W. R. (1995). Do bridges exist between psychophysics and neurophysiology? In P. R. Killeen & W. R. Uttal (Eds.), *Fechner Day 1999: Proceedings of the 15th Annual Meeting of the International Society for Psychophysics* (pp. 1–22). Tempe, AZ: ISP.

Uttal, W. R. (1998). *Toward a new behaviorism: The case against perceptual reductionism.* Mahwah, NJ: Lawrence Erlbaum Associates, Inc.

Valkenburg, O. H., Hauf, P., & Sarris, V. (2000). *Asymmetry and frequency effects in time perception.* Unpublished manuscript quoted after Hauf (2001).

Von der Heydt, R., & Peterhans, E. (1989). Mechanisms of contour perception in monkey visual cortex: I. Lines of pattern discontinuity. *Journal of Neuroscience, 9,* 1731–1748.

Von der Heydt, R., Zhou, H., & Friedman, H. S. (2000). Representation of stereoscopic edges in monkey visual cortex. *Vision Research, 40,* 1455–1967.

Von der Heydt, R., Friedman, H. S., & Zhou, H. (2003). Searching for the neural mechanism of color filling-in. In L. Pessoa & P. De Weerd (Eds.), *Filling-in: From perceptual completion to cortical reorganization* (pp. 106–127). Oxford: Oxford University Press.

Vonhausen, R., Szczepansky, M., Hauf, P., & Sarris, V. (1998). Altersspezifische Genese multidimensionaler Objektwahrnehmung in Abhängigkeit von Instruktion und Stimulusmaterial. [Age-specific development of multidimensional object perception as a function of instruction and stimulus material.] In H. Lachnit, A. Jacobs, & F. Rösler (Eds.), *Experimentelle Psychologie: Abstracts der 40. Tagung experimentell arbeitender Psychologen* (p. 271). Lengerich, Germany: Pabst.

Von Hofsten, C. (2002). On the development of perception and action. In J. Valsiner & K. J. Connally (Eds.), *Handbook of developmental psychology* (pp. 114–140). New York: Sage.

Von Hofsten, C. (2004). An action perspective on motor development. *Trends in Cognitive Sciences, 8,* 266–272.

Von Uexküll, J. (1934/1957). The world of animals and men. In C. H. Schiller (Ed.), *Instinct behaviour: The development of a modern concept* (pp. 5–81). New York: International Universities Press. [Translated from J. von Uexküll, 1934: *Streifzüge durch die Umwelten von Tieren und Menschen.* Berlin: Springer.]

Wagner, A. R. (2003). Context-sensative elemental theory. *Quarterly Journal of Experimental Psychology, 56B,* 7–29.

Wallach, H. (1948). Brightness, constancy and the nature of achromatic colors. *Journal of Experimental Psychology, 38,* 310–324.

Walsh, V., & Kulikowski, J. (Eds.). (1998). *Perceptual constancy: Why things look as they do.* Cambridge: Cambridge University Press.

Walsh, V., & Pascual-Leone, A. (2003). *Transcranial magnetic stimulation: A neurometric of mind*. Boston, MA: MIT Press.

Ward, L. M. (1973). Repeated magnitude estimation with a variable standard: Sequential effects and other properties. *Perception and Psychophysics, 13*, 193–200.

Ward, L. M. (1979). Stimulus information and sequential dependencies in magnitude estimation and cross-modality matching. *Journal of Experimental Psychology: Human Perception and Performance, 5*, 444–459.

Ward, L. M. (1987). Remembrance of sounds past: Memory and psychophysical scaling. *Journal of Experimental Psychology: Human Perception and Performance, 13*, 216–227.

Ward, L. M. (1990). Critical bands and mixed-frequency scaling: Sequential dependencies, equal-loudness contours, and power function exponents. *Perception and Psychophysics, 47*, 551–562.

Ward, L. M. (1992). Mind in psychophysics. In D. Algom (Ed.), *Psychophysical approaches to cognition* (pp. 187–249). Amsterdam: North-Holland.

Ward, L. M. (2002). *Dynamical cognitive science*. Cambridge, MA: MIT Press.

Ward, L. M. (2003). Metapsychophysics: Some "big" questions and tentative answers. In B. Berglund & E. Borg (Eds.), *Fechner Day 2003: Proceedings of the 19th Annual Meeting of the International Society for Psychophysics* (pp. 337–342). Stockholm: ISP.

Watt, R. (1988). *Visual processing: Computational, psychophysical, and cognitive research*. Hove, UK: Lawrence Erlbaum Associates Ltd.

Watt, R., & Phillips, B. (2005). The function of dynamic grouping in vision. *Behavioral and Brain Sciences*. (In press.)

Wearden, J. H., & Ferrara, A. (2004). Stimulus range effects in temporal bisection. *Quarterly Journal of Experimental Psychology, 49B*, 24–44.

Wedell, D. H. (1985). Contrast effects in paired comparisons: Evidence for both stimulus-based and response-based processes. *Journal of Experimental Psychology: Human Perception and Performance, 21*, 1158–1173.

Wedell, D. H. (1996). A constructive-associative model of the contextual dependence of unidimensional similarity. *Journal of Experimental Psychology: Human Perception and Performance, 22*, 634–652.

Wedell, D. H. (2004). Range-frequency prototype model of judgment and discrimination. *Perception and Psychophysics*. (In press.)

Weintraub, D. J. (1975). Perception. *Annual Review of Psychology, 26*, 263–279.

Wertheimer, M. (1959). On discrimination experiments: I. Two logical structures. *Psychological Review, 66*, 252–266.

Weser, D., Arlt, M., & Sarris, V. (2000). Contextual shifts in time-perception judgments depending on different methods. In C. Bonnet (Ed.), *Fechner Day 2000: Proceedings of the 16th Annual Meeting of the International Society for Psychophysics* (pp. 369–374). Strasbourg: ISP.

West, R. L., Ward, L. M., & Khosia, R. (2000). Constrained scaling: The effect of learned psychophysical scales on idiosyncratic response bias. *Perception and Psychophysics, 62*, 137–151.

Westheimer, G. (1999). Gestalt theory reconfigured: Max Wertheimer's anticipation of recent developments in visual neuroscience. *Perception, 28*, 5–15.

Wilkening, F. (1976). *Entwicklungspsychologische Experimente zur Wahrnehmungs- und Urteilsrelativität*. [Developmental experiments on the perceptual and judgemental relativity.] Meisenheim a.Gl., Germany: Hain.

Wilkening, F. (1982). Children's knowledge about time, distance, and velocity inter-relations. In W. J. Friedman (Ed.), *The developmental psychology of time* (pp. 87–112). New York: Academic Press.

Wilkening, F., & Anderson, N. H. (1982). Comparison of two rule assessment methodologies for studying cognitive development and knowledge structure. *Psychological Bulletin, 92*, 215 237.

Wilkening, F., & Sarris, V. (1975). Informations-Integration bei Kindern und Erwach-senen: Eine Überprüfung verschiedener psychophysischer Modelle. [Information-integration in children and adults: A comparative test on some psychophysical models.] *Zeitschrift für Psychologie, 183*, 307–318.

Wilkening, F., Levin, I., & Druyan, S. (1987). Children's counting strategies for time quantification and integration. *Developmental Psychology, 23*, 823–831.

Wilkening, F., Sarris, V., & Heller, O. (1972). Contrast effects in the child's judgment of lifted weight. *Psychonomic Science, 28*, 207–208.

Wilson, B., Mackintosh, N. J., & Boakes, R. A. (1985). Transfer of relational rules in matching and oddity learning by pigeons and corvids. *Quarterly Journal of Experimental Psychology, 37B*, 313–332. (Quoted after Pearce, 1994.)

Woodward, A. L. (2003). Infant cognition. In L. Nadel (Ed.), *Encyclopedia of cognitive science* (Vol. 2, pp. 525–531). New York: Nature.

Wright, A. A., Rivera, J. J., Hulse, S. H., Shyan, M., & Neiworth, J. L. (2000). Music perception and octave generalization in rhesus monkeys. *Journal of Experimental Psychology: General, 129*, 291–307.

Wright, A. A., Rivera, J. J., Katz, J. S., & Bachevalier, J. (2003). Abstract-concept learning and list-memory processing by capuchin and rhesus monkeys. *Journal of Experimental Psychology: Animal Behavior Processes, 29*, 184–198.

Yager, R. R. (2003). Fuzzy logic. In L. Nadel (Ed.), *The encyclopedia of cognitive science* (Vol. 2, pp. 176–180). New York: Nature.

Yonas, A. (2003). Development of space perception. In L. Nadel (Ed.), *Encyclopedia of cognitive science* (Vol. 4, pp. 96–100). New York: Nature.

Zadeh, L. A. (2001). Toward a logic of perceptions based on fuzzy logic. In W. Novak & I. Perfilieva (Eds.), *Discovering the world with fuzzy logic* (pp. 4–28). Heidelberg, Germany: Physica-Publ.

Zayan, R., & Vauclair, J. (1998). Categories as paradigms for comparative cognition. *Behavioural Processes, 42*, 87–99.

Zeigler, H. P., & Bischof, H.-J. (Eds.). (1993). *Vision, brain, and behaviour in birds*. Cambridge, MA: MIT Press.

Zemel, R. S., Behrmann, M., Mozer, M. C., & Bavelier, D. (2002). Experience-dependent perceptual grouping and object-based attention. *Journal of Experimental Psychology: Human Perception and Performance, 28*, 202–217.

Zentall, T. R., & Wasserman, E. A. (Eds.). (2005). *Comparative cognition: Experimental explorations of animal intelligence*. (In press.)

Zoeke, B. (1987). Altersspezifische Frequency-Effekte im psychophysikalischen Bezugssystemversuch. [Age-specific frequency effects in the psychophysical frame-of-reference experiment.] *Zeitschrift für Psychologie, 195*, 101–103.

Zur Oeveste, H. (1987). *Kognitive Entwicklung im Vor- und Grundschulalter: Eine Revision der Theorie Piagets*. [Cognitive development in preschool and elementary school age: A revision of Piaget's theory.] Göttingen: Hogrefe.

Author index

Subject index

Note: page references in **bold** refer to tables or figures.